TITLE II-A

The Manuscript Poems of A. E. Housman

The Manuscript Poems of
A. E. HOUSMAN

Eight Hundred Lines of Hitherto Uncollected
Verse from the Author's Notebooks

edited by

TOM BURNS HABER

The University of Minnesota Press, Minneapolis

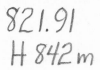
The quotations from *A Shropshire Lad, Last Poems, More Poems,* and *Additional Poems* on pages 19, 23, 24, 33, 36, 40, 42, 44, 45, 46, 49, 52, 54, 57, 58, 59, 62, 63, 64, 68, 69, 78, 80, 81, 85, 88, 90, 107, and 118 are reprinted from *The Collected Poems of A. E. Housman,* copyright 1922, 1940 by Henry Holt and Company, Inc.; copyright 1936, 1950 by Barclays Bank, Ltd. *Additional Poems* was originally included in *My Brother, A. E. Housman,* by Laurence Housman, published by Charles Scribner's Sons, copyright 1937, 1938 by Laurence Housman. All quotations are used by permission of the publishers, the Society of Authors as the literary representative of the trustees of the estate of the late A. E. Housman, and Messrs. Jonathan Cape, Ltd., publishers of *A. E. Housman's Collected Poems.*

FOR GRACE

Preface

THE manuscript poems with which this volume is concerned
are in the following collections: the remains of A. E. Housman's
four notebooks, in the Library of Congress; the printer's copy of
A Shropshire Lad, in the Library of Trinity College, Cambridge
University; and the printer's copy of *Last Poems*, in the Fitzwilliam Museum, Cambridge.

Of the notebook remains, by far the most valuable corpus of
Housman manuscripts, only a minor portion has been dealt with
here in detail: namely, those pages containing new poetry. I have
made frequent reference to the larger portion of the notebook
contents, which consists of drafts and fair copies of Housman's
published verse, but I have not attempted anything approaching
a systematic survey. To deal adequately with this rich material,
nothing less than a full-scale variorum edition will suffice.

Because of the circumstances outlined in Part One, there has
been considerable discussion in the public press about the propriety of using the Housman manuscripts now in the Library of
Congress. After weighing the pros and cons, I do not believe that
there is any valid objection to making the contents of the notebooks available to the public. All legal objections have been
withdrawn, in writing, by Laurence Housman and Barclays Bank
Ltd., the designated trustees. The Library of Congress, in keep-
ing with its long-established policy of neutrality in such matters,
has expressed through its Librarian the opinion that, legal permission granted, the publication of the notebook remains involves

no ethical consideration which might "embarrass the strictest sense of scholarly propriety."

For assistance in the preparation of this volume I am indebted in various ways to the generosity of many persons: chiefly to Mrs. Matthew John Whittall, of Washington, D.C., who purchased the notebook manuscripts and gave them to the Library of Congress and who has provided me with essential information regarding their history; to the Ohio State University Research Foundation for grants-in-aid which enabled me to live with the manuscripts during the summers of 1950, 1951, and 1952; to David C. Mearns, chief of the Division of Manuscripts in the Library of Congress, who made available to me many additional facilities (not the least of which was privacy) during my reading; to Henry B. Dillard, formerly of the Division of Manuscripts, whose love for Housman's poetry led him to make the first complete editorial assay of the reliquiae and whose willingness to extend his working hours into the very late afternoon opened to me a knowledge of the manuscripts I could not have obtained in any other way; to Earle F. Walbridge, editor of the *Papers of the Bibliographical Society of America,* for permission to reprint in Part Five an article published originally in the *Papers*; to Henry Holt and Company, the Society of Authors, London, as the literary representative of the trustees of the estate of the late A. E. Housman, and Messrs. Jonathan Cape, Ltd., for permission to quote from *The Collected Poems of A. E. Housman* and to Charles Scribner's Sons for permission to quote from *My Brother, A. E. Housman.*

T. B. H.

The Talking Trees
Columbus, Ohio
1 September 1954

Chronology of the Manuscripts

NOTEBOOK A

Sept. 1890: Earliest surviving date, written on page 106. (The serious poems began on page 53.)

1893, early months: Unique draft of "A. J. J." on page 161. Housman's friend, A. J. Jackson, died 12 November 1892.

March 1895: Latest surviving date, written on page 237, five pages from the end.

NOTEBOOK B

April 1895: Earliest date, written on page 3.

April or May 1895: Last stanza of *LP* 7,* on page 12. (Sir Sydney Cockerell in Laurence Housman's *My Brother, A. E. Housman,* page 275, dates *LP* 7 in April 1922, except for the final stanza, "written long previously.")

6 August 1895: Date of the event commemorated in *ASL* 44, written on pages 60–65, August or September.

August or September 1895: First draft of *AP* 18, on pages 70–71. (This poem is thought to express Housman's feelings on the condemnation of Oscar Wilde, May 1895.)

Dec. 1895: Latest date, written on page 116, prior to the publication of *A Shropshire Lad.*

1900 or earlier: Draft and fair copy of *LP* 4, on pages 191–92. This poem was first published in *Academy,* 24 February 1900.

1901–2: Second draft, on pages 200–1, of the dedicatory Latin poem to

*Throughout this volume, in identifying specific poems, the four sections of Housman's poetry are referred to by these symbols: *ASL, A Shropshire Lad; LP, Last Poems; MP, More Poems; AP, Additional Poems.*

M. J. Jackson, published in Volume I of Housman's edition of Manilius, 1903.

After October 1901: Unique draft, on page 215, of *MP* 40, written in commemoration of the death of Housman's brother, George Herbert.

7 June 1902: Latest date, written on the final page, 231. (The date is of the publication of "The Olive" (*AP* 23); the page was probably written soon *after*.)

NOTEBOOK C

No dates survive in this notebook.

1917 or earlier: First and second drafts of *LP* 37, on pages 92–93. This lyric first appeared in the *London Times*, 31 October 1917, on the third anniversary of the first battle of Ypres.

NOTEBOOK D

10 April 1922: Earliest surviving date, written on page 76. (Most of the preceding pages probably date within this month.)

May, June 1922: Latest entry written for *Last Poems* (number 18), on page 108.

19 June 1922: Printer's copy of *Last Poems* sent to Grant Richards.

Jan. 1925: Latest surviving date, written on page 112. (The remaining thirteen pages were probably written within a few months.)

30 April 1936: Death of A. E. Housman.

26 October 1936: Publication of *More Poems* (London: Cape).

1937: Publication of eighteen *Additional Poems* in *My Brother, A. E. Housman,* by Laurence Housman (London: Cape).

1939: Publication of *The Collected Poems of A. E. Housman* (London: Cape); first collection of *Additional Poems* 19–23.

1939–40: Seven portions of the notebook remains and other poetry manuscripts purchased by Mrs. Matthew John Whittall, of Washington, D.C., and presented to the Library of Congress.

5 and 12 June 1943: First publication, by John Carter, of erased and canceled variorum matter (of *MP* 4), in the *London Times Literary Supplement.*

1945: Notebook manuscripts cleaned of adhesive and remounted, making accessible 136 portions of concealed writing.

1947: Complete collection microfilmed.

1952–53: The four notebooks reconstructed by the present editor.

The Notebooks and the Library of Congress Manuscript Collection

Library of Congress Manuscript Collection	Notebook A (87 pieces)	Notebook B (92 pieces)	Notebook C (21 pieces)	Notebook D (44 pieces)
Volume I*				
Volume II (Sheets 1–43)	Sheets 1–43 (complete volume except piece 1 on Sheet 38; total 70 pieces)	Sheet 38 (piece 1)		
Volume III (Sheets 44–97)	Sheet 79 (one piece) Sheet 80 (three pieces)	Sheets 44–97 (complete volume except four pieces on Sheets 79, 80; total 90 pieces)		
Volume IV (Sheets 98–106)		Sheet 106 (piece 2)	Sheets 98–106 (complete volume except piece 2 on Sheet 106; total sixteen pieces)	
Volume V (Sheets 107–33)	Sheet 133 (pieces 2, 3, 4)		Sheet 133 (piece 1)	Sheets 107–32 (complete volume except four pieces on Sheet 133; total forty-three pieces)

* Volume I includes Explanatory Remarks; Table of Abbreviations; Indexes locating the poems in the collection; Inventory of the remaining seven volumes page by page.

Library of Congress Manuscript Collection	Notebook A (87 pieces)	Notebook B (92 pieces)	Notebook C (21 pieces)	Notebook D (44 pieces)
Volume VI (Sheets 134–50) †				
Volume VII (Sheets 151–57)	Sheets 151, 152, 156 (two pieces each) Sheet 157 (one piece)		Sheets 154, 155 (two pieces each)	Sheet 153 (one piece)
Volume VIII (Sheets 158–65) ‡	Sheets 158, 160, 165 (one piece each)			

† An inventory of this volume is given on pages 4–5. All these sheets are foolscap size, written on one side only. The poems are rejects from *A Shropshire Lad* and *Last Poems*.

‡ Volume VIII includes in addition "As into the Garden Elizabeth Ran" (Sheet 159); "Fragment of an English Opera" (Sheets 161–62); and "Their Substantives in Gender, Number, and Case" (Sheets 163–64).

Contents

The Manuscript Poems of A. E. Housman

PART ONE

The Notebooks

HISTORY

THE most valuable of A. E. Housman's literary remains are the surviving portions of his notebooks, now in the Library of Congress, in which he composed and copied nearly all the poems published under his name. From these notebooks he selected the contents of *A Shropshire Lad,* which appeared in February 1896, and *Last Poems,* published in mid-October of 1922.

Nearly fourteen more years of reasonably active life remained to him after the second slim volume was issued, but in that period he composed only a handful of new poems and showed no inclination to produce a third book from the once- and twice-winnowed pages of his notebooks. These manuscripts passed nearly intact into the hands of Laurence Housman after his brother's death on the last day of April 1936.

Some years before that event, A. E. Housman had concluded that he would not forbid the posthumous publication of some of his recent poetry or of the material he had himself passed over in assembling *A Shropshire Lad* and *Last Poems.* His will, dated 19 November 1932, bequeaths all his books and manuscripts to his brother, with the proviso (section 7) that Laurence must "destroy all my prose manuscript writing in whatever language." The section continues, "And I permit him but do not enjoin him to select from my verse manuscript writing and to publish any poems which appear to him to be completed and to be not inferior in quality to the average of my published poems."

Whether or not Laurence Housman was acquainted with the exact language of this section of his brother's testament before A. E. H. died, he was aware of the nature of the responsibility he was expected to assume and on at least one occasion, two years prior to his brother's death, pressed him to do some dividing between the sheep and the goats.[1] But from Laurence's published statements it may be inferred that A. E. H. indicated few if any preferences or discards among the reliquiae of his four notebooks. Additional selections remained for the brother-executor to make —well, badly, or not at all.

However, within the manuscripts left to him Laurence found some new material that stood out above the rest:

1. Separate from the notebooks there were seventeen foolscap sheets containing fifteen poems that had been copied for possible inclusion in *A Shropshire Lad* or *Last Poems*.[2] The unpublished pieces, nine in number, even though they bore the stigma of rejection from one or the other of the two volumes, would have had a high priority in Laurence's esteem, for they must have reminded him that A. E. H. himself had published in *Last Poems* a few lyrics once intended for his first book but thrown out of printer's copy or proof sheets at the eleventh hour. Among the nine foolscap pieces there were at least five rejects from the pre-final assembly of the copy of *Last Poems*. All but one of the new poems eventually appeared in the first posthumous collection, *More Poems* (1936).[3]

---

[1] *My Brother, A. E. Housman* (New York: Scribner's, 1938), p. 114.

[2] The history of these rejected pieces is given in more detail in Parts Four and Five of the present volume, where the printer's copies of *A Shropshire Lad* and *Last Poems* are described.

[3] These seventeen sheets now occupy Volume VI of the Library of Congress collection. Three were once in the printer's copy of *A Shropshire Lad*:

"Yonder see the morning blink" (*LP* 11)
"In the morning, in the morning" (*LP* 23)
"The Sage to the Young Man" (*MP* 4), two sheets

There are three other sheets that evidently belong with these early castoffs. They are written in the same style and on the same kind of ruled paper:

"Easter Hymn" (*MP* 1)
"Oh who is that young sinner . . . ?" (*AP* 18)
"I promise nothing: friends will part" (*MP* 12)

The remaining ten sheets are quite different from the rest: the writing is more erratic and sketchy; the paper shows a very faint horizontal rule and a heavy

The Notebooks

2. Within the notebooks themselves Laurence found a number of complete unpublished poems unscored by any of the numerous rejection signs A. E. H. sprinkled liberally throughout his pages. In the shrunken form of the notebooks as they now exist, twenty-four such poems may still be identified; nineteen of these appeared in *More Poems* or in the augmented section of *Additional Poems* in the comprehensive edition issued by Cape in 1939. The remaining five will be found in this volume.

I have said that the notebooks were *nearly intact* when Laurence Housman received them. At least one sheet was missing, the one containing the final lyric of *A Shropshire Lad,* which the poet himself destroyed to prevent posterity from solving a riddle he had set his listeners in his Leslie Stephen lecture, "The Name and Nature of Poetry."[4] He described how the stanzas of *ASL* 63 came to him one after the other, implying in his account that he composed them in an order different from that in which they were eventually published. Some came easily, others were difficult: could his listeners now tell which were which from reading the poem? This owlish conundrum provoked some inquiry and may eventually have involved A. E. H. deeper than he wished. But he was a past master at putting a stopper on curiosity and in this matter he was obdurate. He never revealed his secret, trifling as it intrinsically was; and before taking leave of his notebooks he saw to it that the telltale page which carried the story of the composition of *ASL* 63 did not survive to betray him.

It should be remembered, then, that when Laurence Housman sat down over his brother's papers he found therein but few spe-

---

left-margin rule in red ink. The nine poems contained in these sheets—there are two drafts of "Smooth between sea and land" (*MP* 45)—were being groomed for *Last Poems,* but only four passed into printer's copy as the following catalog shows:

"In midnights of November" (*LP* 19)
"I counsel you beware" (*MP* 26)
"As I gird on for fighting" (*LP* 2)
"The night my father got me" (*LP* 14)
"Smooth between sea and land" (*MP* 45)
"Sinner's Rue" (*LP* 30)
"The Land of Biscay" (*MP* 46)
"Delight it is in youth and May" (*MP* 18)
"On forelands high in heaven" (*MP* 33)

[4] See *The Name and Nature of Poetry* (Cambridge: Cambridge University Press, 1950), pp. 49–50.

cific guides to assist him in the selection of new material for publication. There were the nine poems on the foolscap sheets and at least twenty-four unblemished pieces in the notebooks, but these were too few to make a worthwhile *annexe* to what A. E. H. had already sent forth. If anything of sufficient substance was to appear, there must be a heavy draft on the canceled poems in the notebooks, and in choosing among these Laurence had to face the simple and difficult terms of section 7 of his brother's will, which may have been not untinctured with malice. What is the "average" of the poems in *A Shropshire Lad* and *Last Poems*? And what divinity can say of one particular unpublished lyric that it is or is not "inferior to the average"? The lot of a prospective editor confronted by these questions is not a happy one, and Laurence's difficulties in arriving at the answers are on record in his prefaces to *More Poems* and *My Brother, A. E. Housman,* in which *Additional Poems,* containing eighteen pieces, first appeared, in 1937.

In his Preface to the first of these volumes, after quoting the pertinent section of his brother's will, the editor continues: "The responsibility which has thus been laid on me is of a double character; for while I am anxious to include nothing that can do hurt to my brother's literary reputation, I am most reluctant to deprive his lovers of any poems, however minor in character, which are not inferior to others—also minor in character—which have already been published. . . .

"My main difficulty has been this: that while I would naturally wish to give any poem of minor merit the benefit of the doubt, and am therefore inclined to err on the side of leniency, I know well that his own decision would be more likely to err on the side of severity. But since in only one case has he crossed out a finished poem with the written comment 'not good,'[5] it would seem that he intended to leave all the rest freely to my own judgment —average merit and completeness being the limiting conditions.

"Several of these poems, as were some of *Last Poems* also, are of *Shropshire Lad* date, and though the name of 'Terence' . . . does not reappear, it is evident that a good many,[6] especially

---

[5] The notebook page bearing this poem has not survived.

[6] A numerical analysis may be useful here. From page 27 to page 48 of *More Poems* there are 21 pieces (nos. 10–30). Of these, only half belong to the "Terence

6

those from page 27 to page 48, belong to the Terence series . . ."[7]

Laurence Housman finally selected forty-nine pieces for *More Poems*—just over half of the candidates that awaited his decision. Notebook A contained usable drafts of sixteen pieces that went into this volume; B, nine; C, four; and D, eighteen. This apportionment I make from a survey of the notebooks as I have reconstructed them from photographs. Possibilities of error lurk in this estimate, for some pieces of *More Poems* were apparently drawn from notebook pages that no longer exist; and the published texts of others may have been based on drafts found in two or more notebooks. Two of the lyrics—*MP* 5 and *MP* 48—were never drafted in the notebooks or in the other manuscript remains and must have been supplied by outside sources.

The principal divisions of *My Brother, A. E. Housman* are (1) the 104-page Memoir, (2) eighty pages of letters, (3) the group of eighteen *Additional Poems,* and (4) the page-by-page Analysis of the more than 600 notebook pages containing serious poetry. In his Introduction the editor returns to the theme which he had discussed at some length in his Preface to *More Poems*:

"My responsibility both of inclusion and exclusion in the editing of those left-over poems was very great, and in more instances than one I could find no satisfactory solution. Had I added a larger number, either of short pieces, single stanzas, or verses of a minor quality, their inclusion might have done harm to the selection as a whole. But, though it includes one poem which I would now rather have omitted, *More Poems* has in the estimation of most of its critics done its author's reputation no disservice; and in consequence I now feel myself more free to give separately in this memoir a few remaining pieces, about the publication of which I was in the first instance doubtful." (Page 15.)

In his Note on the *Additional Poems* Laurence, without mentioning his brother's will, again refers to his editorial responsibilities and makes a distinction between this fourth corpus of his brother's poetry and the three that preceded it: "But as the three books of published poems may now be regarded as constituting

series," for no more than eleven were written in the notebooks before the copy of *A Shropshire Lad* went to the printer.

[7] A. E. H. at one time had intended to name his first book *The Poems of Terence Hearsay.*

the canon of my brother's poetry, I feel myself freer to make these few additions. . . ." (Pages 211–12.)

Of the eighteen pieces of *Additional Poems,* Notebook A supplied two; B, ten; C, one; and D, two. Numbers 5 and 13 were never represented in the notebooks; number 18 was drawn from one of the foolscap sheets described on page 4. The extreme dates of the poems in this issue, as of those in the preceding one, are widely separated: *AP* 12 was copied by A. E. H. on page 61 of Notebook A long before the first date entered in the notebook (September 1890), and *AP* 14 is found for the first time on page 97 of D, which almost certainly was written in April 1922.[8]

When *Additional Poems* was incorporated into the one-volume comprehensive edition published by Cape in 1939, this section was augmented by five pieces, making the total number twenty-three. Four of these new pieces either had appeared or were about to appear in periodicals; only number 20 was generally unknown prior to the issuance of the *Collected Poems.* Sources outside the notebooks furnished the texts of numbers 19, 20, and 21; number 22 had been written on A 214–15, and number 23 on B 229–31.

Interesting as these eighteen poems are, of even greater interest to students of the poetry as a whole is Laurence Housman's Analysis of the contents of the notebooks, which by his tally summed up to about 650 pages. This index was no small task. He began, it would seem, by numbering the pages of each book.[9] Then he tabulated the poems and fragments on 188 pages of A; 231 pages of B; 112 pages of C; and 125 pages of D. He located rough drafts or fair copy, or both, of every poem but ten of the 177 now in the *Collected Poems.* Two of the unnoted ten pieces —*LP* 26 and *LP* 32—were actually in the notebooks, but for some reason Laurence ignored them.[10]

---

[8] There are signs that this may be a copy of an earlier draft, although the Analysis of Notebook D indicates that pages 97 and 98 (the latter has not survived) contained a "rough draft and fair copy" of this poem. No other reference to it is given in the Analysis.

[9] The numerals now at the top of the pages evidently were not made by A. E. H. All are in pencil, even those on pages written only in ink; furthermore the numbering seemingly was not done as each new page was opened but was added after the pages were inscribed. This is evident particularly on pages with no top margin, where the numerals were crowded in wherever the writing left room for them.

[10] *LP* 26 was on D 86; *LP* 32 on D 73. Both of these notebook pages survive.

The Notebooks

It should be remarked finally that the Analysis was made with something less than the accuracy its subject demanded. Certainly, A. E. H. would have found in it ample reason for displeasure —reason beyond the mere fact of its existence. Laurence set about making the Analysis knowing that considerable portions of the notebooks would be destroyed;[11] the Analysis alone would preserve the main features of the complete record. But there are many unfortunate lapses: some pages that yet survive are described in the Analysis as containing drafts they never received; other pages show poems that the Analysis does not mention. Again, some pages—for example, D 86, 87, 88, 89, which contain fair copies of *LP 26*, *MP 33*, and *LP 21*—are completely passed over. The numbering is often erratic, two pages sometimes receiving the same numeral or a full-written page not being numbered at all. Anyone relying confidently on the Analysis throughout is certain to be misled. For some data it is, unfortunately, our only source; but wherever possible its testimony should be weighed with other evidence.

After *Collected Poems* was published in 1939, it was expected that the four notebooks, as A. E. H. had left them, would cease to exist. Would they disappear entirely? The order for destruction, it should be remembered, did not apply to the manuscripts of published poems; and all of this material Laurence Housman was naturally anxious to preserve. There were difficulties in the way, however, for most of the notebook leaves contained writing on both sides, and savable material was inextricably mixed with contraband on page after page. Only about sixty sheets were "pure." In order that no workshop sketching or other interdicted verse should ever pass under other eyes, these precautions were taken:

1. Many whole sheets—about 140—were removed, and portions of as many more were cut out and destroyed. In this latter process, sometimes only two or three consecutive lines of a full page were excised, leaving the sheet in two sections; sometimes more cutting was done on a single leaf, with the result that the material remaining was in three or even four sections; or a full sheet might be reduced to a single scrap no larger than a postage

---

[11] See *My Brother, A. E. Housman*, pp. 251-52.

stamp. When all these reductions had been made, the approximately 650 pages of the notebooks had shrunk to about 402, counting both cut and uncut pages.[12]

2. The ink and pencil drafts of many fragments and of some poems published and unpublished were erased or heavily canceled. This obliteration in ink and pencil seems to have been done after the leaves of the notebooks had been separated and after the excisions had been made, for some of the ink cancel strokes near the top and bottom edges of some page fragments appear to have been made with a more deliberate hand than would have been necessary if the pen had been moving freely over a full page.[13]

3. At this time or later all the surviving notebook material, complete leaves and tiny fragments, was attached to new mounting sheets. There was contraband manuscript on only one side of practically all the pieces now—pieces containing it on both sides had gone to the fire—and this side was pasted down, leaving exposed fair copy or drafts of poems that did not vary much from the printed versions.[14]

In these operations the sequence of the notebook pages was completely overturned. It is difficult to say whether in the beginning it was intended to be kept. True, the first few pages of Notebook A as it now exists in the second volume of the Library of Congress collection roughly parallel the opening entries of the Analysis; but this correlation, if it was designed, was soon lost in a maze of widely separated sheets and juxtaposed pages that bore little or no relation to each other in date or content. Thus two fragments of A 125 were put on mounting sheets now numbered

[12] This more than one-third loss of material does not mean that some 250 written pages were lost. Of the 402 whole or partial pages that remain, twenty-seven are blank; it is probable that an even greater proportion of blank pages were among the sheets destroyed.

[13] This is not to say that all of the erasures and cancellations must be charged to a later hand than the poet's. To make a reliable chronological distinction in every case is impossible, but there seems to be no doubt that A. E. H. erased many passages himself. He also employed at least six different types of cancel strokes and used all of them most effectively at times.

[14] There were a few exceptions to this method. Some of the mounts contained single sheets, hinged, with penciled notations identifying the stanzas on the under side; others contained two or more such sheets overlapping each other. Obviously, nothing but published material was displayed on mounts thus set up.

80 and 152; four fragments that eventually came to rest on sheet 106 originally belonged with pages C 43, B 226, C 48, and C 49.

Nevertheless, after all the cutting and reshaping, the notebook remains included in one form or another, ranging from rough draft to fair copy, all but 20 of the 177 poems now found in the *Collected Poems*. Of *A Shropshire Lad* there were all but numbers 41, 54 (the latter apparently never in the notebooks), and 63 (removed by A. E. H. himself); of *Last Poems* all but 14, 30, and 37; of *More Poems* all but 5 and 48 (these two never in the notebooks) and 19, 22, and 45; and all of *Additional Poems* but 5, 13, 19, 20, and 21 (none of these in the notebooks) and 1, 2, 6, and 7. Thus of the twenty unrepresented poems, eight should not be counted as casualties, for they seem never to have been written into the notebooks; of the actual losses, A. E. H. is responsible for one and Laurence Housman for eleven.

As addenda to this body of notebook material, two further sections of manuscripts found among the papers of A. E. H. were assembled and pasted to mounting sheets. The first section, already mentioned, consisted of the seventeen foolscap sheets of poems copied while *A Shropshire Lad* and *Last Poems* were being readied for the printer; the second was a miscellany of humorous verse and prose jottings. In the latter were two and one-half sheets from the earliest section of Notebook A.[15] The mounting sheets, 165 in number, were finally arranged in the following sequence: 1–133, notebook remains; 134–50, foolscap sheets; 151–57, notebook remains; and 158–65, miscellany.

Seven new "books"—lettered from A to F, the seventh unlettered—were formed of these sheets, and in 1939 they were sold, through the agency of London and New York booksellers, to a New York dealer. They were purchased from him by Mrs. Matthew John Whittall, of Washington, D.C., who presented the collection to the Library of Congress.

Even though writing on the affixed sides of the sheets showed through plainly on many of the exposed pages, it was not until

---

[15] "After five pages of epigrammatical sentences, forty-eight pages are alternately occupied by classical notes to the right, nonsense verses to the left"— the description of Notebook A, in *My Brother, A. E. Housman*, p. 256. The surviving sheets are those containing pages 9 and 10, 11 and 12, and 17 and 18 (upper halves only).

1945 that an investigation of the full resources of the collection was undertaken at the suggestion of Robert Penn Warren, then consultant in poetry at the Library. At this time all of the 245 pieces of manuscript that once belonged to the notebooks were detached from their mounting sheets. They were cleaned and remounted, hinged, on the original mounts; and these, together with the foolscap sheets and the miscellany, were finally reassembled within bound volumes (numbers II, III, IV, V, VI, VII, and VIII of the collection) that preserved the identical grouping and sequence of the manuscripts when received in America.[16] (A cross-reference list of the notebook pieces and the contents of the Library of Congress volumes is given on pages ix and x.)

As a result of the exploration of the manuscripts, 136 new sections of poetry were discovered on the verso sides of the notebook leaves. It is from these verso pages that all the hitherto unpublished poetry in Part Two of this volume has been taken.

Anyone setting out to read the story of A. E. Housman's poetical activity as revealed in the notebook remains must sooner or later essay a reconstruction of the notebooks, to put them as nearly as possible in the condition in which they were left at the poet's death. Working with photoduplicates and Laurence's Analysis, he will find this not as difficult as would appear from the "most admired disorder" of the Library of Congress collection as it now exists. The allocation of some waifs and strays among the smaller fragments must be conjectural, but well over ninety per cent of the 244 pieces can be traced back to notebook and page number. The dates which A. E. H. scattered throughout the notebooks, a knowledge of his concordance, familiarity with the varying appearance of his handwriting over the span of thirty-five or forty years—all these factors aid in reshuffling an un-

[16] As was feared, the adhesive had already spoiled the legibility of some of the pieces. The fading on A 84, 113, 144, 239; B 230; D 31, 73, and 106 may be explained thus.

One piece was lost in the reassembly: the lowest of the three originally affixed to the thirty-eighth mounting sheet. It was a fragment of *ASL* 3. Another loss was sustained in the withdrawal of the sheet originally numbered C 7. It appears that this sheet was taken from the collection before it was received by the Library, for the inventory after C 6 reads "C 7 (not included with the collection)." It is hoped that this portion of the notebooks will be restored by its present possessor or at least identified.

numbered piece back to its provenance in the notebooks. The tale of Housman's inner life was written plain in the four books of manuscript poems, and the reconstructed notebooks still contain many of the essential records, plus a wealth of minutiae equally important to the student of the poet's way. These records increase our knowledge of Housman's craftsmanship and at the same time enable us to correct several long-standing misconceptions—some of them planted by A. E. H. himself.

Since the sequence of the manuscript pieces in the Library of Congress volumes is largely fortuitous, the collection in its present form does not serve as a satisfactory page-and-item reference. For this purpose it is necessary to use the reconstruction of the notebooks mentioned above. Furthermore in the following pages, fully mindful of the many lacunae in the reassembled sheets but wishing to avoid belaboring the phrase "in the surviving manuscripts," I have as a rule made no reference to the losses which the original four books have suffered but have simply referred to pages and poems with the reconstructed notebooks in mind.

The Library of Congress has expressed an interest in the further rehabilitation of this valuable collection and in the rectification of errors in the already considerable quantity of editorial work expended upon it (now contained in Volume I); and it is probable that before long those who consult the remains of A. E. Housman's notebooks will find them in a condition of much greater usefulness.

NOTEBOOK A

In his Preface to *Last Poems*, Housman said, ". . . in the early months of 1895[17] I wrote the greater part of my other book . . ." This period marked one high tide of his poetry, and the notebook record for the first five months of 1895 is more complete than for many other less productive periods, which were often marked by a larger quantity of experimental verse. It is on page 216 of A that we first meet the date "Jan. 1895"; and all but the very last

[17] In his reply (February 1933) to M. Pollet's "gimlet questionnaire" A. E. H. narrowed this period down to "the first five months of 1895." See Grant Richards, *Housman, 1897–1936* (New York: Oxford University Press, 1942), p. 271. Also, in the first draft of his Preface Housman had once written "the first five" instead of "early."

one (pages 241–42) of the following sheets of Notebook A have survived in whole or part. The bridge from A to B must have been a short one, for A 237 is scored "March 1895" and B 3 bears in the upper right corner the date "April 1895." The first entry dated June (that date may be taken as the termination of "the early months") appears on page B 36.

Let us see what was done for English poetry in these five months. Twenty-three of the lyrics of *A Shropshire Lad* were drafted, nineteen of them in such a state of finality that they were never rewritten in the notebooks. This is the catalog:

"The Welsh Marches" (*ASL* 28) A 217

"Reveille" (*ASL* 4) A 218–19, two drafts

"The Recruit" (*ASL* 3) A 222–25, two drafts

"On moonlit heath and lonesome bank" (*ASL* 9) A 226–27, two drafts

"The Immortal Part" (*ASL* 43) A 228–29, two drafts

"When I watch the living meet" (*ASL* 12) A 230

"Look not in my eyes . . ." (*ASL* 15) A 232

"The winds out of the west land blow" (*ASL* 38) A 233

"The Day of Battle" (*ASL* 56) A 236–37, two drafts

"Others, I am not the first" (*ASL* 30) A 238

"To an Athlete Dying Young" (*ASL* 19) A 240, B 10–11

"The Lent Lily" (*ASL* 29) B 3

"Loitering with a vacant eye" (*ASL* 51) B 8–9

"This time of year a twelvemonth past" (*ASL* 25) B 14–15

"On your midnight pallet lying" (*ASL* 11) B 16

"Oh, when I was in love with you" (*ASL* 18) B 17, 29

"1887" (*ASL* 1) B 18–19, second draft

"Westward on the high-hilled plains" (*ASL* 55) B 20–21

"The street sounds to the soldiers' tread" (*ASL* 22) B 22–23

"Oh see how thick the goldcup flowers" (*ASL* 5) B 24–25, second draft

"Twice a week the winter thorough" (*ASL* 17) B 26–27

" 'Is my team ploughing?' " (*ASL* 27) B 31–32

"Loveliest of trees . . ." (*ASL* 2) B 33–34, two drafts

It is obvious that most if not all of Housman's familiar themes and characters are in these twenty-three poems: the war-sick soldier, the lovesick youth, patriotism, pastoral beauty, home-sickness, the fate-led end of things. All of these were to be touched again—sometimes with greater vigor or precision, sometimes

14

with an acridity that could come only from wells of life that were poisoned. Still to be developed was the mastery of style that showed itself in the concluding trio of *Last Poems*, with their superb orchestration and their matured sense of pathos.

The first five months of 1895, then, saw the completion or near-completion of twenty-three, but only twenty-three, of the sixty-three poems of *A Shropshire Lad*. To accommodate these facts with Housman's statement that most of his first volume was written during that time would require a very liberal interpretation of the verb *wrote*. Even though the word is taken to mean "compose," difficulties remain; for as a rule after composing his poems during afternoon walks, A. E. H. wrote them down upon returning to his rooms.[18] This is one of the haunting questions that arise when we turn from the Preface of *Last Poems* to the notebook record: what did Housman mean by "early"? He seems not to have been a fluent writer; even his second and third drafts are often labored. He told his audience in his Leslie Stephen lecture that he wrote the last poem of *A Shropshire Lad* thirteen times. Was he indulging in some comfortable exaggeration when he said the "greater part" (his first draft of the Preface[19] had "three-quarters") of *A Shropshire Lad* was done in the opening months of 1895? Or must we imagine that many—perhaps twice twenty-three—of the lyrics of that volume were written not where we should expect to find them, in the last twenty-six pages of Notebook A and the first thirty-six pages of Notebook B, but on loose sheets that are now lost or scattered? Some poems, we know, were never drafted in any of the notebooks, but these are few, only eight or nine; and it does not fit with our knowledge of Housman's meticulous care of his papers to think that he would fail to put many poems in the treasury with the others. Until other evidence appears, it seems clear that we must question his statement of the fruitfulness of the early months of 1895.

How many *Shropshire Lad* pieces had been done before the high tide of that year? The testimony of Notebook A is eloquent

[18] In his *Name and Nature of Poetry* (pp. 48–49) after describing how the poems flowed into his mind he continues, "When I got home I wrote them down. . . ."

[19] This manuscript is now in the collection of A. B. Collamore, of Hartford, Connecticut.

here: from page 53, where the serious poems begin, to page 216 (dated "Jan. 1895"), A. E. H. finished or nearly finished eighteen lyrics that went into his first volume and began two or three others that were completed in Notebook B. There is an unmistakable air of completeness about these eighteen pieces; actually, eight of them had attained the finality of ink copy years before Housman's first volume had a name, and no fewer than sixteen of them were never retouched prior to the composition of printer's copy.

It is well known from sources outside the notebooks that the writing of some of the pieces of *A Shropshire Lad* antedated the publication of the book by many years. Percy Withers, for example, reported that Housman told him that the first poems were composed in 1886.[20] Thus from more than one kind of evidence it is plain that a considerable part—about one third—of Housman's first volume was down on paper before the onset of "the continuous excitement" which overwhelmed him in the opening months of 1895. The high tide was preceded by a long swell; and we shall see that there was an equally long ebb.

The first *Shropshire Lad* poem is on A 63; it is "Into my heart an air that kills" (number 40). The second is on A 82–83, "There pass the careless people" (number 14); the third is on A 84, "Bring, in this timeless grave to throw" (number 46). The latter is a rough pencil draft that shows signs of fresh composition, but the first two are ink drafts and, even though corrected, indicate that they were not composed there but were copied from loose sheets or a notebook antedating A. To continue the list from A 84, the following lyrics were written before the end of 1894:

"The Merry Guide" (*ASL* 42) A 106–9, 114–15, three drafts

" 'Tis time, I think, by Wenlock town" (*ASL* 39) A 125, 153, 155, fair copy

"Bredon Hill" (*ASL* 21) A 132–33, 142–43, fair copy

"Far in a western brookland" (*ASL* 52) A 134–35, fair copy

"From far, from eve and morning" (*ASL* 32) A 144–45, 158, fair copy

"Be still, my soul, be still . . ." (*ASL* 48) A 146–47, 159, fair copy

"If truth in hearts that perish" (*ASL* 33) A 148, 164–65

"You smile upon your friend to-day" (*ASL* 57) A 164

[20] See *A Buried Life* (London: Cape, 1940), p. 67.

The Notebooks

"March" (*ASL* 10) A 170
"White in the moon the long road lies" (*ASL* 36) A 181
" 'Farewell to barn and stack and tree' " (*ASL* 8) A 191
"The Isle of Portland" (*ASL* 59) A 192
"Hughley Steeple" (*ASL* 61) A 193
"1887" (*ASL* 1) A 202–3
"As through the wild green hills of Wyre," six lines (*ASL* 37) A 204
"The Recruit," two stanzas (*ASL* 3) A 205, 222–25
"Now hollow fires burn out to black" (*ASL* 60) A 207
"Oh see how thick the goldcup flowers," last 11 lines (*ASL* 5) A 208
"The True Lover" (*ASL* 53) A 210–13, fair copy

One more word on the opening section, pages 54–105, of the first notebook: This part may have been originally something of a continuation of the miscellany which began with page 1, described by Laurence Housman in the preface to his Analysis as containing epigrammatical sentences, classical notes, and nonsense verses. Our knowledge of pages 54–105 is woefully imperfect, for only one of the sheets has survived uncut and fifteen have been destroyed completely. The dates of the drafts from page 54 on seem not to follow regularly the sequence of the pages in the reconstructed notebook; for example, the fragment on A 87, in its content and penmanship, seems to antedate the clear ink draft of *MP* 3 on A 58–59; and this draft, in turn, seems not to be contemporary with the lines traced in now-faded ink on the opposite side of the sheet. It may be conjectured that the twenty-six sheets of the first section of A were filled slowly over a period of several years. Then, after inked copies of possibly juvenile poems had been entered here and there, intervening pages were filled with fragments of experimental verse—some, stanzas in sequence; others, single lines. This freehand sketching would naturally be the first to fall before the scissors when the notebooks came to judgment, and it is not surprising that only one sheet has escaped uncut. But the heavy losses in this small area of Notebook A look heavier still when it is discovered that of all the remaining pages, 106 to 241, only thirteen whole sheets perished.

Page 106 of A marks a dividing line in Housman's poetry, perhaps in his life. From this point onward the notebook ceases to be a copybook and becomes a composition book. The preceding page has its own mystery; it contains nothing but the word "Delos" neatly traced in pencil near the top center. Whether this solitary name was to have been followed by a poem or by a series of lecture notes, we shall probably never know; but there is no doubt that the poetic fire fell between the writing of "Delos" and the turning of the page, for A. E. H. from 106 onward was absorbed heart and soul in "The Merry Guide" (*ASL* 42). One nearly complete draft of the fifteen-quatrain poem filled A 106–7, and he immediately proceeded to write his second draft on the next two pages. Then he turned back to a poem, "The Sage to the Young Man," which he had broached years earlier on A 54, and filled pages 110 and 111 with an ink-and-pencil draft of it. The next two pages received some experimental verse, mostly canceled later, and then *ASL* 42 was resumed and brought to near-perfection on 114–15. Opposite the last stanza, A. E. H. penciled "Sept. 1890"—the date he had set near his title "The Merry Guide" on A 106.

There is no doubt that September 1890 marks the start of the "continuous excitement" that produced *A Shropshire Lad*. After A 116 the poems cluster thick. Dashing off second and even third drafts, Housman completed *ASL* 21 ("Bredon Hill"), 52 ("Far in a western brookland"), 32 ("From far, from eve and morning"), 48 ("Be still, my soul be still . . ."), 33 ("If truth in hearts that perish"), 39 ("'Tis time, I think, by Wenlock town") —all within the space of A 125 to 165. "The Sage to the Young Man" was the most troublesome—or at any rate got the most attention. After reverting to it on A 110–11, A. E. H. took it up again on page 136, filled that page and the next with a full draft, turned the leaf and copied another on 138–39; on A 176 he was at it again and began a final ink draft on A 177 (where it first received a title, "The Wise Man to the Young Man"), completing the poem on page 179. After so much effort to bring this poem about, it must have required a measure of abnegation for A. E. H. to throw it out of the proof sheets of his first volume. But he knew, like others of his race, that poetry does not always follow labor.

An important event in Housman's life—the death of his friend A. J. Jackson, 12 November 1892—is recorded on A 161. This page, headed by the initials "A. J. J.," which served for a title when the poem appeared as *MP* 42, is filled with a much-corrected draft of the poem, which A. E. H. never copied.

Among the fragments are occasionally found single lines or couplets that later were wrought into a poem engendered by the provocative idea in the fragment or by the language of it. For example, the germ of "Along the field as we came by" (*ASL* 26) is in two lines jotted down on A 192:

> And she shall lie with earth above
> And you beside another love.

"Soldiers marching, all to die" on A 220 was the genesis of "On the idle hill of summer" and became line 8 of the poem (*ASL* 35). The last two lines of "Westward on the high-hilled plains" (*ASL* 55) were once penciled and erased at the top of A 221:

> And the youth at morning shine
> Makes the vow he will not keep.

But almost as often afterthought was destroyer rather than preserver, and thus we sometimes find single lines and stanzas canceled out of fully developed poems. A comprehensive list of these rejections is given in Part Three of this volume.

The size of the sheets in Notebook A is 5⅛″ x 8″. Of the original 187 pages following number 54, about 80 pages (if we total all missing full sheets and fractions of clipped sections) have been lost. Generally speaking, the majority of the whole sheets that survive contain on at least one side drafts of well-known poetry and therefore escaped the "abhorrèd shears"; the destruction was greatest among the pages containing fragments, but the surviving pages of this kind were seldom written full and the versos were sometimes blank. Thus we may rest in the belief that not a large percentage of writing and no important poems in Housman's first notebook have perished.

Notebook A contained enough first-rate poetry to make its author famous if B, C, and D had never been written. In it, finished or in various stages of completion, were 68 of the 177 pieces we now read in *Collected Poems*: 39 from *A Shropshire Lad*, 5 from *Last Poems*, 19 from *More Poems*, and 5 from *Additional Poems*. There was no stopping, however, at the end of A 241, for that page was written when the high tide of poetry was at the full and could not be held back.

NOTEBOOK B

The second notebook, the largest of the four, records the climax and all but the very end of A. E. Housman's creative energy. When he wrote out fair his copy of "The Olive" on B 231, the harvest was nearly all in; only some thirty new poems—and no more than a handful of these could be named among his best— were yet to come from his pen. Of the forty-two pieces of *Last Poems,* which was not to appear until twenty years later, two thirds were on paper by the time the final page of Notebook B was inscribed.

The pages of the second book measure $4\frac{1}{4}''$ x $6\frac{3}{4}''$. Somewhat as Notebook A divides at page 106, B has its line of demarcation at page 117. The entries up to this page are obviously a continuation of the work that began on A 106: there is the same clear rapid penmanship of fair copies crowding on the heels of first and second drafts, the familiar evidence of the "continuous excitement" that produced *A Shropshire Lad.* Most of the poetry written on these pages of Notebook B was done to stay: it was redrafted with but few essential changes, if any, and went on into the texts for all to read. Consequently there was little to tempt destruction here, and from page 1 to 117 no more than fourteen whole sheets have been lost and of these, six pages were probably blank.

Just as an examination of the early pages of Notebook A proved that about a third of Housman's first volume was done before the opening of the *annus mirabilis,* 1895, so it is evident in B that another third saw the light after the months that he said were so productive. Actually the month of August seems to have been the richest of all. The date "August 1895" is written on B 53, and all of twenty-seven well-filled pages stretch between it and the first page dated "September 1895."[21] In these pages Housman

[21] It must be granted that these two dates may not actually define the amount of work done in August, since no *days* are given. Thus some pages before B 53 may have also been written in August, just as some written before B 80 may belong with September's work. It seems reasonable to believe, however, that A. E. H. would have entered in his notebooks the name of a month about the

brought to completion, or near it, the following pieces of *A Shropshire Lad*—some of them among his finest:

"The Carpenter's Son" (47)
"As through the wild green hills of Wyre" (37)
"The winds out of the west land blow" (38)
"Shot? so quick, so clean an ending?" (44)
"If it chance your eye offend you" (45)
"Reveille" (4)
" 'Is my team ploughing?' " (27)
"The Immortal Part" (43)
"When smoke stood up from Ludlow" (7)
"Oh fair enough are sky and plain" (20)

Of the above, number 44 was written three times, and 45 and 20 were brought into fair copy. Also done in August were two drafts of "Oh who is that young fellow . . .?" (later *AP* 18) and a fair copy of "Her strong enchantments failing" (once intended to be 43 of *A Shropshire Lad* but withdrawn from proof sheets, eventually to become *LP* 3).

In the pages from 80 to 116 the name of each remaining month in the year is entered, but they are not widely separated in the sparse record; for example, in October only one entry seems to have been made—a second draft (on B 95) of "In midnights of November" (*LP* 19). It is on page 116 that we find "Yonder see the morning blink" (two drafts), which was once ranked with the printer's copy of *A Shropshire Lad* but rejected at the last minute. The poem later passed as number 11 of *Last Poems*.

By the time B 116 was written, printer's copy of Housman's first volume of poetry had been completed. The high tides of inspiration had subsided, and the next few pages are filled with the flotsam of the ebb. Some portions in the latter part of B show, even over a dozen or more consecutive pages, the old confident hand; but the quantity of uninspired writing must have been large if we may judge only from the number of sheets that have perished. The letdown immediately following B 116 must have been striking, for every page between it and B 136 went to the

time of the arrival of the first day. Reckoning all probabilities, we may believe that the August harvest was in quantity as well as in quality the richest of this rich year.

fire; and on down to the end of this book forty-one sheets have been lost as against fourteen missing from the first part. Laurence Housman's obit in the Analysis for the majority of these later items is "Single lines and fragments." Practically all the completed poems were new ventures; only once, it would seem, did A. E. H. turn back to Notebook A to review and finish a poem begun before *A Shropshire Lad* was turned out. This was "The fairies break their dances" (*LP* 21), which was carried forward from A 125 to B 161.

Our understanding of how the latter part of Notebook B was composed is greatly hampered by the fact that A. E. H. entered but one date in it after page 116, and that was on the final page: "7 June, 1902," above a fair copy of "The Olive" (*AP* 23). This chronological peg is, as it happens, of very little use, for it dates not the draft of the poem but publication in *The Outlook*. More abundant but not much better help may be found in a few dates furnished by Housman's close friend Sir Sydney Cockerell on information derived from the poet himself. But Cockerell's dates, which are given in Laurence Housman's Memoir (pages 274–75), are often inexact—for example, "c. 1900–1905"; "soon after 1900"; "before 1904"; etc.—and need to be checked against other data.

The closely written pages of Notebook B, with its numerous rough drafts, reveal many glimpses of Housman's methods of composition. His approach to the lyric that became number 7 of *Last Poems* is of particular interest. The first sign of it in the notebooks is on B 12, where amid a maze of other fragments A. E. H. penciled this quatrain in April or May 1895:

> And you with colours gay
> And martial music swelling
> Walk the resounding way
> To the still dwelling.

Perhaps eight or nine years later A. E. H. took up the theme again on B 176. How much was done this time can only be guessed, as the middle third of the page has been cut out. But at the top of the lower fragment may be read the line "And both are sighing"—the last line of the penultimate stanza. About twenty years afterward the poem was taken in hand again and fair copy written on D 53. The lone stanza composed nearly three decades earlier on B 12 now became, with some alterations, the conclusion of the poem.

The two drafts of "This time of year a twelvemonth past" (*ASL* 25) on B 14–15 afford an amusing example of the poet's indecision with proper names, which were often a topic for self-debate. In the printed text the name of the girl over whom the rival lovers quarrel is Rose Harland. But in the first draft of his poem A. E. H. gave the name Harland not to the maiden but to the Shropshire Lad's rival:

> Ted Harland, fourteen months ago,
> When he and I would meet . . .

In the second draft the rival becomes Fred Loughton, but he is still named Ted in the last stanza!

Laurence Housman's Analysis for B has it that pages 204 and 205 contained a rough draft of three stanzas of "The Deserter" (*LP* 13). Page 205 has not survived and the only relic of the first version of *LP* 13 is a single quatrain standing alone at the bottom of B 204:

> Kiss your girl and then forget her;
> 'Tis like the brave:
> They love the leaden bullet better
> To sleep with in the grave.

This was rewrought to become the concluding stanza of the poem:

> "Sail away the ocean over,
> Oh sail away,
> And lie there with your leaden lover
> For ever and a day."

To propose a generalization which the examples just given and the abandoned passages in Part Three will support: the alterations made by A. E. H. between his first drafts and printer's copy indicate that one prevailing principle in his revising was the tendency to move from the direct and explicit to the indirect and implicit.[22]

---

[22] This is a subject which awaits fuller consideration. In addition to the two

The final pages of Notebook B were written during the Boer War, in which Housman became personally engaged following the enlistment of his youngest brother, George Herbert. The latter's death, 30 October 1901, is commemorated in "Farewell to a name and a number" (*MP* 40), written on B 215, and "The Use of the Globes" (*LP* 17), renamed "Astronomy," written on B 221. Some of the stanzas of "The rain, it streams on stone and hillock" (*LP* 18) may also refer to the same event, although the poem seems to have been begun prior to it.[23]

NOTEBOOK C

Originally the smallest of the notebooks, C has suffered losses greater in proportion than the damage inflicted on any of the other three. Of its 112 pages but 30 remain today, and of this remnant 16 pages exist only in fragments of various sizes, and 2 are blank. After page 50, 23 sheets were destroyed en bloc—a single loss not paralleled in any other notebook. The quantity of freehand, experimental writing in Notebook C would, as with the

examples given above, two more may be cited. Line 21 of *ASL* 4 passed through these revisions on A 219:

1. Lads were born to play the rover
2. Feet were wrought to play the rover
3. Stones lie still, but blood's a rover
4. Clay lies still, but blood's a rover

The fifth stanza of *ASL* 9 at one time read thus on A 227:

> And helpless to the hangman's noose
> In blue of morn will go
> A neck I'd keep for kinder use
> Than break it for a show.

The bluntness of the last two lines was softened in printer's copy to

> A neck God made for other use
> Than strangling in a string.

A systematic study of Housman's notebooks will also reveal how often he turned for aid to alliteration and how often it betrayed him.

[23] The last stanza of *LP* 18, apparently the first one written (B 144), certainly does not refer to the death of George Herbert; nor does "Illic Jacet" (*LP* 4), which was written on B 191–92 and published in *Academy*, 24 February 1900. Both of these poems, therefore, are tours de force despite their sense of acute personal involvement.

The idea of a soldier's burial is an obsession with A. E. H. that developed through the second notebook. The earliest record is on B 8, headed "The Soldier's Grave," with the solitary line near the bottom "But he must lie alone."

material in the latter portion of B, be the warrant for extensive destruction. The size of the sheets in C is 3⅞″ x 6⅜″.

Housman left no dates in Notebook C as we now have it, but from internal evidence and from the few dates supplied by Sir Sydney Cockerell we may judge that he began it about 1902. The inspiration that produced his first volume had long since run its course, there was no renewal of the "continuous excitement," and the poetic afflatus touched the latter pages of Notebook C more and more rarely. Hence arises a likely reason for its brevity: A. E. H. may have abandoned his third notebook a few years after he began it. The weakening of his creative energies may have made him declare to himself, as he so often had to others, that he would write and publish no more. As he turned down page 112 of his third notebook he may have felt he was writing his farewell to poetry. When many years later he decided to bring out *Last Poems* and began collecting material for it, it would have been natural to pass over any blank pages remaining within the dusty covers of Notebook C and begin a new fourth book.

The third notebook was nevertheless the depository of a few significant pieces and contributed its quota to *Last Poems*. Six numbers that went into that volume were carried from Notebooks A and B into C and there brought to, or near, fair copy:

"Lancer" (*LP* 6) C 15–16, 19–20
"Spring Morning" (*LP* 16) C 29–30
"The sigh that heaves the grasses" (*LP* 27) C 33
"Now dreary dawns the eastern light" (*LP* 28) C 49
"Revolution" (*LP* 36) C 14, 18
"Fancy's Knell" (*LP* 41) C 6–7

Eight more of the lyrics of *Last Poems* were begun in Notebook C:

"Could man be drunk for ever" (*LP* 10) C 4
"Eight O'Clock" (*LP* 15) C 96–99, fair copy
"When the eye of day is shut" (*LP* 33) C 45–46
"When summer's end is nighing" (*LP* 39) C 28, line two only

(According to Laurence Housman's Analysis this latter poem was continued on C 90–91, but the sheet of these pages has been destroyed, as have been the sheets for the following.)

"We'll to the woods no more" (*LP* Prologue) C 89, 107
"Wake not for the world-heard thunder" (*LP* 29) C 70–71
"Hell Gate" (*LP* 31) C 81
"Epitaph on an Army of Mercenaries" (*LP* 37) C 92–93

Finally, this notebook once contained the unique drafts of two pieces of *More Poems,* besides the drafts, more or less complete, of six others that were published in that volume. The second lyric of *Additional Poems* also was taken from C 94–95 (the only draft, since destroyed).

Another unique feature in this notebook is a line begun with the ending evidently in mind but left incomplete in the middle of a word. On C 44 Housman was composing "Delight it is in youth and May," which was eventually to become *MP* 18. He traced the opening words of the fourth line of stanza two: "Is he . . ." and stopped. Nothing else was written on the lower half of the page. The line later developed into "Is heard beneath the hill"; but one wonders what the importunity was that halted the flying pen thus abruptly. Weariness? . . . the signal bell? . . . a person from Porlock?

NOTEBOOK D

Most of the fourth book—all but a few of the first 54 sheets—was written in one month, April of 1922. The first date to appear in its 125 pages is "10 April 1922," inscribed in the upper right corner of D 76. The size of the pages in this book is $5\frac{1}{4}''$ x $8\frac{3}{8}''$.

Notebook D is mainly a copybook, a collection of poems begun in the three earlier notebooks and passed over as unworthy or unfinished when the material for *A Shropshire Lad* was being assembled. I have spoken of D as being a "new" book, but it seems probable that long before April 1922 Housman had been writing in it *juvenilia* and fragmentary verse. Only a half-page (of number 91) of this kind of material has survived, but it is enough to show a striking contrast to the contents of the surrounding pages.[24]

A. E. H. wrote only fifteen new poems in Notebook D and used but six of these in *Last Poems*:

"Soldier from the wars returning" (*LP* 8) D 22

[24] See the fragment and the note on page 91 of this volume.

The Notebooks

"When I would muse in boyhood" (*LP* 32) D 73
"The half-moon westers low, my love" (*LP* 26) D 86
"The night is freezing fast" (*LP* 20) D 90
"The sloe was lost in flower" (*LP* 22) D 99
"Tell me not here" (*LP* 40) D 100–1, the latter page lost[25]

This evidence, which is unmistakably plain in the reconstructed notebook, can hardly be made to fit with Housman's statement in his Preface to *Last Poems* that "About a quarter of this matter belongs to the April of the present year," unless *belongs to* is taken to mean "was copied in." Even though Housman's longest poem, "Hell Gate" (begun late in Notebook C), adds its bulk to the work of April 1922, the total is a considerable distance short of a fourth of the contents of *Last Poems*. A simple tally of the forty-two pieces of his second book shows that sixteen were carried over into Notebook D from one or more of the earlier books,[26] and twenty others never were transcribed on the pages of D at all, printer's copy being written from the drafts in A, B, and C. In claiming so much for April 1922 Housman may have been using the same exaggeration he risked when in the same Preface he said that the greater part of *A Shropshire Lad* was written in the early months of 1895. His first draft of the Preface contained this more ample phrase, referring to one fourth of the contents of *Last Poems:* "belongs to the present year." A. E. H. would have been nearer the truth if he had expanded the time limit even farther.

Housman had been importuned in many quarters to bring out a second volume of his poetry but had always put off his advisers with various excuses, alleging nearly all but the main one: that there was not enough in his notebooks to make a worthy successor to *A Shropshire Lad*. Whatever it was that caused him to alter his decision, it was made sometime before 5 September 1920. On that date, writing to his publisher, Grant Richards, he inquired: "Suppose I produced a new volume of poetry, in what

[25] The drafts of only two of these pieces—*LP* 22 and *LP* 32—show signs of fresh composition. The unique draft of *LP* 8 is a fair copy, in ink, further evidence that A. E. H. did not always begin composing his poems in the notebooks.

[26] The farthest return was to A 125, where one stanza of "The fairies break their dances" (*LP* 21) had been written in, or shortly after, September 1890. Four other pieces that went into *Last Poems* were drawn, more or less complete, from the first notebook: numbers 3, 12, 19, and 24.

part of the year ought it to be published, and how long would it take after the MS left my hands?"[27] Housman threw out the warning four months later that the new book was not at all a sure prospect, and Richards did not know until 9 April 1922 that it would be ready that autumn.

It is well to bear in mind that A. E. H. made the inquiry of his publisher knowing that a new volume, if he produced one, would no doubt have to consist mainly of poetry written many years before. He knew, as he states in his Preface, that there would be no revisitation of the moods that produced *A Shropshire Lad*. It should be remembered, too, that in the year and a half between his first hint to Richards and the opening of Notebook D he produced little or nothing. One might almost contend that it was the stimulus of copying the rejected work of other, better years that inspired the little new material that did come from his pen. And in saying this one should at the same time say that one lyric written fire-new for *Last Poems*, "Tell me not here," sounds depths of tenderness and beauty that *A Shropshire Lad* did not achieve.

There is a depressing methodicalness about the surviving pages of Notebook D. The clean, carefully traced ink drafts that fill page after page are dull reading after tasting the conflict that left its mark on the desperate interlineations and cancel signs in A and B. Of the 71 pages remaining in the fourth book, 57 were written in ink; and 28 of these latter are duly marked with the long vertical line which A. E. H. struck through them as one by one he garnered them into his printer's copy. Poetry and book-keeping are equal partners.

The first nine sheets of D have perished, but Laurence Housman's Analysis records that two copies of the Introduction to *Last Poems* occupied the first two pages. The last poem entered in the fourth notebook prior to the making of printer's copy was "The rain, it streams on stone and hillock," which became *LP* 18. This lyric, begun well over twenty years before on B 144, and taken up again on B 175, was probably readied for the book only at the very last minute. It had been a stubborn holdout all through the crowded April of 1922, resisting three previous attempts in D to bring it about. The final struggle on D 107 and

[27] See Richards, *Housman, 1897–1936*, p. 178.

108 seems to have ended before victory, for the two stanzas on the fragment of page 107—all of the draft that has survived—are filled with corrections. A. E. H. must have written and destroyed more than one subsequent draft of *LP* 18 before he worried out the text that Grant Richards read on June 20.

After A. E. H. turned page 108 of his fourth notebook, he did not lay it aside forever. Sixteen more pages were written in D, of which eight whole pages survive, together with the upper halves of two others (116, 117). Number 112 is the first of the entire pages, and it contains the only completely new poem Housman wrote in this final portion of his last book. It was printed as *MP* 47. Below the date "Jan. 1925"[28] Housman inscribed this heading:

For my funeral
to the tune of *Brief life is here our portion.*

Page 113 now shows a partly decipherable quatrain, written in ink and heavily overscored with ink.

The sheet containing pages 114 and 115 has been destroyed. The fragment of page 116 contains the "Dream poem" and a prose note (see page 93 of this volume); the verso carries a fair copy of *MP* 37, which A. E. H. brought forward from C 50 (lost).

Page 118 is occupied by the "Beech Tree" lyric, which is printed on page 94 of this volume. The four stanzas written in ink are now heavily canceled in the same medium, but it seems a fair surmise that A. E. H. at one time regarded this poem as having a claim to survival equal to that of the funeral poem on D 112. Neither page is scored in the upper right corner with the stigmata A. E. H. so often used to remind himself and others of a poem's inferiority—an X followed by a trailing line. The cancellations of the "Beech Tree" poem resemble the wavy ink strokes that apparently were made in the notebooks after May 1936. The poem itself may contain echoes from Propertius (I, xviii).

The next four pages seem to have been written with the idea of posthumous publication firmly fixed in the poet's mind. They contain, in this order, fair copies of *MP* 21, *MP* 6, and *MP* 34, all brought forward from earlier drafts in the notebooks. Except for

---

[28] None of the poems following bear dates, but from the uniformity of the ink drafts that comprise the bulk of the second portion it would seem that only a few weeks or months separated pages 112 and 123.

two lines in the second stanza of *MP* 34 on D 121, practically every line in these three lyrics is unblemished. They must have been among the first of the elect for *More Poems*.

The final sheet, bearing pages 124 and 125, went to the flames; and so the verso of D 122 is the latest survivor. It presents an ink draft of "Crossing alone the nighted ferry" (*MP* 23), corrected with pencil and scored with the X-and-trail, but uncanceled. This lyric, thoroughly pagan, is as characteristic of the poet as the one he wrote on D 112 to the tune of a church hymn; and these two pieces, beginning and closing the last section of his notebooks, in a manner symbolize and sum up the two parts of A. E. Housman's inner life. Those who put their trust in symbols may also find it worthy of remark that the last phrase we now read in his last notebook is "the grave."

❦ PART TWO ❧

Poems and Fragments

THE verse contained in this section is printed to reproduce as closely as type allows the display and position of the lines as they appear on the manuscript pages. Alternative readings that were canceled are generally not given; all uncanceled alternatives, unless insignificant, are shown.

The following signs have been used to mark omissions and doubtful readings in this section and in Part Three:

[   ] indicates the location of a blank space in an unfinished line or stanza.

[?   ] indicates an illegible passage.

The space between brackets approximates that in the manuscript. If there are reasonable grounds for conjecture in the reading of an erased or canceled section, my reading is given, followed by an interrogation sign and enclosed in brackets.

NOTEBOOK A

Date: ? before September 1890

PAGE 60, the upper two thirds

Faded ink, beneath wavy cancellation in heavy ink.

> Nor break my heart with hoping any more,
>> Tomorrow you shall have the grave to wife:
>> Now, in the accepted time, make friends with life.

> To have missed no chances when you come to die
>> Haste, for the heaven is westered since you came:
>> Day falls, night climbs, the hour has lost its name;
>> Quick, quick! the lightning's pace were weary, slow,
>> And here you loiter spelling gravestones: go.[1]

---

[1] Even though this fragment, in tone and content, seems to belong with Housman's *juvenilia,* it is to be noted that the first three lines of it strike the same note sounded in "Because I liked you better" (*MP* 31) and other controversial lyrics published by Laurence Housman, in which estrangement between men is the theme.

Date: ? before September 1890

PAGE 66, nearly complete; two sections
The script of the upper section is in pencil, beneath wavy cancellation in pencil. In the second section, the three lines on the left are in ink; all four lines are canceled in ink.

Heard in the hush of heaven

As often under sighing oak
drowsing
Or near musing hidden laid
Maiden and youth in whispers spoke,
In whispers, youth and maid.[2]

[And scatter the skies with pearl.][3]

Are underfoot to tread

The weapons of the war

The land they perished for.   Lies the defended land.

The soul you died to save[4]

---

[2] This quatrain may represent the beginning of the theme that emerged in "The True Lover" (*ASL* 53), which A. E. H. began on A 210.

[3] The brackets are in the manuscript.

[4] The four lines in the lower section seem to be the preliminaries to "1887," the poem which was to become number 1 of *ASL*. Cf. *ASL* 1, line 24, "The land they perished for," and line 16, "Themselves they could not save." This poem began to take shape on A 202–3.

PAGE 67, complete

Faded ink, beneath wavy cancellation in ink.

Some air that swept the Arabian strand
When the great gulf was calm,
Some wind that waved in morning land
The plumage of the palm.

With odours from the graves of balm
That far away it fanned,
And whispering of the plumy palm
It moved in morning land.

They come: all heaven cannot contain[5]
The [   ]

Cold is the cannon's mouth,
The trumpet's throat is dumb

Never, or ever, shine or snow,
That son of God I used to know.

[5] This line and the word following are in pencil, erased.

PAGE 78, upper third
Pencil, beneath wavy cancellation in pencil; the page overscored with a large **X**.

She would not peace at all; she would not honour
  At all: the Lord hath lifted up therefor
The darkness of his countenance upon her
  And given her war.

        And seas ungoverned of God.

      Hills sky-splintered with thunder
       And towns sea-swallowed of God.[6]

---

[6] This couplet is an early and admirable example of Housman's long-lived fondness for compound epithets. See Grant Richards, *Housman, 1897–1936*, pp. 432–33.

Date: ? before September 1890

PAGE 81, middle half

Ink and pencil.

The upper portion of the piece is filled with an ink draft of the last ten lines of the poem that became *AP* 11, "God's Acre." These lines in the fourteenth impression of the *Collected Poems* (London: Cape, 1953) are mistakenly, I believe, set off as a separate poem.

—The thing that never is again.[7]

    the house that none rebuild[8]

—Where down upon the bed he lies[9]

[7] Lines 1 and 3 were written in ink, later heavily overscored with a wavy cancel line in ink; line 2 was written in pencil.

[8] Cf. "The rain, it streams on stone and hillock" (*LP* 18), lines 21, 22, written on B 144:

> But oh, my lad, the house is fallen
> That none rebuild again.

[9] Cf. "Bring, in this timeless grave to throw" (*ASL* 46), line 21: "Where low upon the couch he lies" (A 84).

These three lines are valuable for what they suggest of Housman's method. They are not alternatives for the poem written over them, but they carry its tone and meaning —sparks from the furnace, so to speak. Two of them were never extinguished and, one a few days later, the other after several years, came to life in other poems.

PAGE 87, upper third

Ink, beneath wavy cancellation in ink; large X overscore. Penciled corrections between lines and in both margins.

The Rights of Men [10]

	Ho, sons of old oppression	
Toiling	Which toil with hardened hands	
	Till the night fall:	
	Good tidings, bond and thrall!	
	Whate'er the	Grudge not the
Whatso	All that all lords of lands	Leave to the lords of lands
	Had ever for possession,	Their perishing possession
	You shall have all.	

The kings whose realms you reap in

---

[10] This is the first surviving instance of the use of a title in the notebooks. Housman's manuscripts, from first draft to final copy, contain many titles for poems that appeared in print untitled.

PAGE 90, upper two thirds
Ink, beneath wavy cancellation in ink.

> The fights they waged aforetime
> Their souls in hell rehearse;
> They have made an end of wartime
> And now they reap the curse.

> The old deceived diviner
> Awakes in hell to find
> The web of doom spun finer
> Than any mortal mind;[11]

---

[11] These quatrains are separated by an inch, and it is possible that they were not considered as parts of one poem. The second, in content and structure, is suggestive of "Her strong enchantments failing" (*LP* 3), which was begun on page 205 of this notebook, some time after the middle of 1894.

PAGE 131, complete
Pencil, erased and overscored with a large X.

    Till fainting the goal you win
    Where Virtue shares the throne with Sin.[12]

There let it lie, son, strike not again:[13]
They do not [sorrow?] for their slain.

               [   ] their strife;
               Long is it, but it ends with life.

[12] Cf. the stanza possibly intended for "The Sage to the Young Man" (*MP* 4), printed on page 97 of this volume. According to Laurence Housman's Analysis the first serious poem represented in Notebook A was "The Sage to the Young Man"; there were at least four drafts of this lyric in the first notebook.
[13] Above this couplet were written two lines now almost illegible.

PAGE 141, complete
Pencil, partly erased; beneath wavy cancellation in pencil; large X overscore.

And from the sky's end the far-journeyed curse
  Is come with its terrible travelling flame.

Faints from ill without

In days when it was gold

Therefore I will not fear, though the solid earth be shaken[14]

he shall not arise[15]

Oh happy he that hears it

Amidst the weaving wrung her hands
  And wept upon the loom of life.

The shepherd shall behold

That never friends the brave[16]

---

[14] Similar echoes of this figure, biblical in origin, are frequent in Housman's poetry; for example, the phrase "earth's foundations" occurs six times.

[15] This may be a return to the theme begun on A 84 and resumed on A 116, where "A Winter Funeral" (*ASL* 46) was drafted, ending

> Where low upon the couch he lies
> Whence he never shall arise.

[16] It is possible that this line is the germ of "As I gird on for fighting" (*LP* 2), the last stanza of which A. E. H. wrote on B 6, April or May 1895 (first draft):

> So here are things to think on
> That ought to make me brave
> As I tie on for battle
> My sword that will not save.

40

PAGE 152, middle two thirds
Pencil, much erased and canceled.

Who squanders and saves in season
   May have the thing he had:
The gift there's no regaining,
   Why will you lose it, lad?

Where have you [had?] the poison
   That your fool's heart is fain
To throw the thing away
   You never have again?

But what you mean to squander
But what men part with liefest
   Twice it was never had
   Will never twice be had:
The gift there's no regaining,
   Why will you lose it, lad?[17]

What light to light the way
               dawn
               heaven
How much more light than morning
   That soul alive bestows
They know not that possess it
   But he that lost it knows.[18]

---

[17] The first three stanzas have the ring of "The Sage to the Young Man" (*MP* **4**).
[18] The compacted gall of this quatrain is the essence of A. E. H.

PAGE 156, complete
Both quatrains in pencil; the first intact, the second erased and canceled with pencil wave.

> I have desired to die,
>   That so this fire might cease,
> When you were lost, and I
>   Were perished and at peace.[19]

> Heard in the hour of pausing voices,
>   That brings the turning wheel to stand,[20]
> When barges moor and windows glisten,
>   And lights are faded in the land.

---

[19] These lines may commemorate Housman's grief at the death of his friend A. J. Jackson, 12 November 1892. His most significant tribute, "A. J. J." (*MP* 42), was written a few pages later, on A 161.

[20] Cf. the opening lines of *MP* 19:

> The mill-stream, now that noises cease,
> Is all that does not hold its peace.

PAGE 162, complete
Pencil, much corrected; erased and line-canceled.

> My heart, my heart is silent,[21]
>   The larks sing loud and shrill.
> High, high the larks hang singing,
>   My heart, my heart is still.
>
> High spring the leaves and grasses,
>   Then I was no more proud;
> My heart, my heart is silent
>   Although the larks sing loud.

Soldier, I wish you well.[22]

> And one remembers and forgets,[23]
>   But 'tis not found again,
> Not though they hale in crimsoned nets
>   The sunset from the main.

---

[21] This and the following quatrain are drawn from two groups of canceled and superscribed lines.

[22] This line was used as the conclusion of *ASL* 22, which was completed (in two drafts) on pages 22 and 23 of Notebook B in May 1895.

[23] This quatrain is the last stanza of "Give me a land of boughs in leaf" (*MP* 8). Stanzas one and two of the poem may have been composed on A 163, of which only two small pieces have survived.

Date: between February 1893 and August 1894

PAGE 163, a scrap (2″ x 3″) cut from the middle of the sheet
Pencil, unerased and uncanceled.

> How many milestones more to pass
> Before the turning road
> Shall bring me to my roof of grass
> And steeple-gloomed abode?[24]

---

[24]Compare with *ASL* 48, particularly the last line, "Oh why did I awake? when shall I sleep again?" Housman began this poem on page 146 of Notebook A, completed the second draft of it only four pages before the place where the above quatrain is written.

Date: between February 1893 and August 1894

PAGE 166, upper half, and PAGE 167, middle half
Both pages in pencil; the first page heavily canceled and overwritten.

These two pages were occupied by the first draft of an unfinished poem, perhaps thirty lines long, beginning, "Come, soldier, to the fight." After this exhortation follows a description of how "in all the sky the shuddering drums begin" and the answering call of the bugle and the neighing of the horses. Midway in the poem the tone of defeat is sounded in the phrases "We shall not win," and " 'Twas lost or ever you and I were man." Again the soldier is exhorted to battle, "where strength is vain and courage nothing can." At the top of the remnant of page 167 are these lines (unerased) that conclude the fragment:

> A weary while ago the world began,
> But oh, this fight was lost before.[25]

[25] Cf. "The Defeated" (*AP* 19), lines 3 and 4:

> And over the dead men roar
> The battles they lost before.

PAGE 176, upper third

Pencil, much corrected; erased and canceled.

> That now are easy found
> Where aye will under the belfry sleep
> Its many-slumbered ground.

> They all were scattered, far to seek,
> That now are easy found
> Where aye the headstone shadows streak
> Their many-slumbered ground.[26]

[26]In spite of some metrical discrepancies these may be experimental drafts of a stanza intended for "The Sage to the Young Man" (*MP* 4). The final copy of this poem follows and takes up pages 177 and 179.

The opening line of the first quatrain above was not written. "They" in stanza two may refer to the opening lines of the stanza at the top of A 179:

> Others, or ever thou,
> For yonder height were sworn.

Cf. *MP* 4, lines 21, 22.

Date: Summer 1894

PAGE 187, upper half

Pencil, unerased and uncanceled; a large X scored across both columns.

No better light than yours   the night-roofed land

[   ] and against my cheek   It blows the blinding sleep
  Flutters
Blows faint the nighted wind[27]

                                        far-beholding hill[28]

[27] This is Housman's first use of the interesting word "nighted." Later, on page 91 of Notebook B, he wrote it into a stanza which eventually became number 3 of *MP* 15: "Beneath him, in the nighted firth," etc. His only other uses of the word were in the opening line of *MP* 23, first drafted on page 59 of Notebook C (the page has been lost) and again on the very last page (123) that has survived in his final notebook: "Crossing alone the nighted ferry," etc.

[28] Cf. "The Land of Biscay" (*MP* 46), line 4: "far-beholding foreland."

PAGE 192, complete
The upper half is filled with "The Isle of Portland" (*ASL* 59). All but two of
the other lines are erased and overscored with wavy cancel lines; all in pencil.

                              Nor the best lads the fondest lovers

And thick the night was snowing

And she shall lie with earth above
And you beside another love.[29]

Young men in love are not to trust

                              When Adam first the apple ate
                              He had a friend to keep him straight;
                              God to a wife: 'twas hopeless odds.
                              Friends are a deal more help than gods.

[29] This couplet (unerased) was evidently the germ of "Along the field as we came
by" (*ASL* 26) and became lines 9 and 10 of the poem. No other notebook entry of this
poem has survived. About ten months after jotting down these two lines Housman
wrote probably the complete twenty lines of the poem on page 36 of Notebook B.

PAGE 194, complete

Pencil, much corrected; beneath wavy cancellation in pencil; large X overscore.

Ned Lear and I were drunk last week,
   dripping
Oh, crying drunk were Ned and I,
Too drunk to see, too drunk to speak,
   helpless   reason
Too senseless drunk to wonder why.
            looked   Ludlow
You might have walked through Wenlock fair
      spied tipsier
And never seen a sillier pair.

         on
   To Ludlow fair, the first of May,
    Two lovely lads
All spic and span went I and Ned
         blue breastknots, neckties gay,
Clean shirts, new ties as blue as day,
New coats on back, new hats on head.
     this week are
And who may now be wearing those
Two
New hats, the Lord Almighty knows.[30]

[

              ] then began
The quarrel which should go with Fan.

[30] Cf. "Terence, this is stupid stuff" (*ASL* 62), lines 29 and 30:

    Oh I have been to Ludlow fair
    And left my necktie God knows where.

A. E. H. had written a few couplets of this poem on pages 187–89 of Notebook A. He completed it on B 84–88, September or October 1895.

He called me all the names he knew,
   that was
And many more than he could spell;
I told him things to think of too
And all about his sister Nell
 And Martin Hughes, and what folks thought
And folks expected: then we fought.[31]

[31] Six years or more later Housman copied the first eight lines of this poem on C 8. (Of the fourth line only the first word was written.) The missing portions of the poem have not been identified; it may be one of several named "unpublished" in Laurence Housman's Analysis.

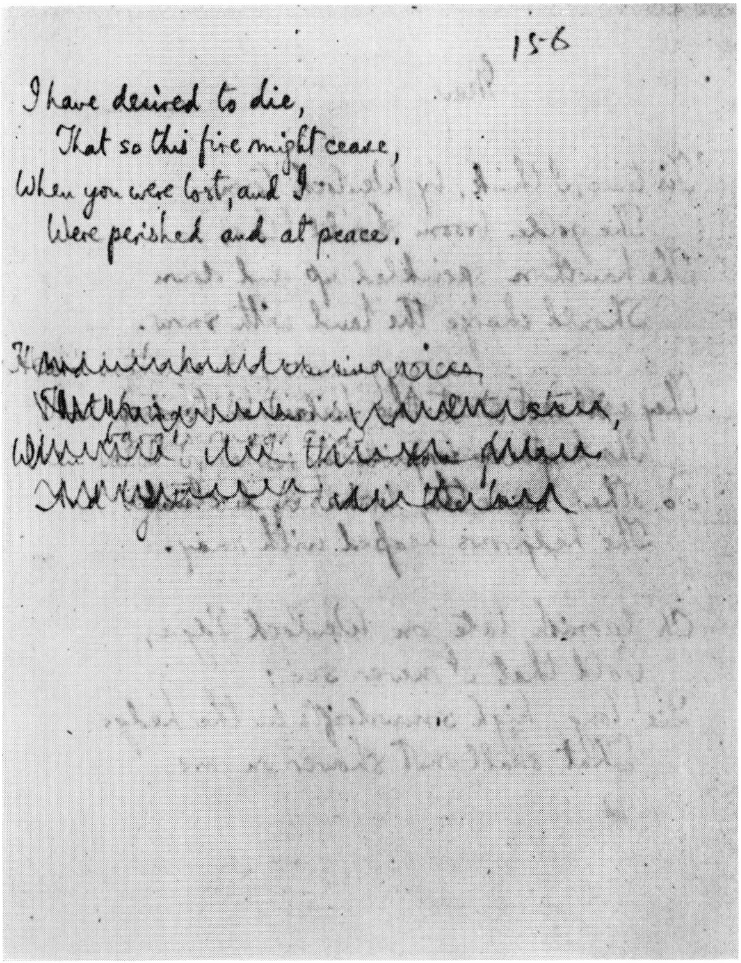

156

I have desired to die,
That so this fire might cease,
When you were lost, and I
Were perished and at peace.

Page 156 from Notebook A: One of the Rare Specimens of Uncanceled Manuscript

PAGE 220, nearly complete; two sections
Pencil, beneath wavy cancellation in pencil; large X overscore.

Soldiers marching, all to die[32]

       Home for us there's no returning[33]

Lovely lads and good to see.[34]   Men that know not day from night
                           Nor their left hand from their right[35]

     The sign-post on the height
       Strikes with five arms to all the sky:
       'Here I go left, and you go right;
         Shake hands, my lad; goodbye, goodbye.'

     [?   ] while the tribes of Genghis Khan
       On Asian mountains moulder in the rain,
   How light upon the desert caravan
     [?   ] the death of Tamerlane?[36]

Hear the silent moon no more
Hale the starring seas ashore.

        Here no hand on all the farm
        Rouses at the false alarm.[37]

[32] This became line 8 of "On the idle hill of summer" (*ASL* 35), first drafted on page 94 of Notebook B, September or October 1895.

[33] Cf. "The Oracles" (*LP* 25), line 15: ". . . and home there's no returning." This poem was written on B 202 about eight years later.

[34] Cf. "Lovely lads and good to know," line 8 of the poem on B 42 (*q.v.*).

[35] This is an early manufacture of the barbed criticisms of various scholarly colleagues, for whom worse punishment was prepared in the trenchant lines on B 199. They are to be found on page 88 of Laurence Housman's Memoir.

[36] Compare the exotic flavor of this quatrain with that of the fragment on A 67, "Some air that swept the Arabian strand." These pieces represent an undeveloped phase of Orientalism in Housman, akin to one that found more complete utterance in poems on themes from Hebrew history: "The Carpenter's Son" (*ASL* 47), "Easter Hymn" (*MP* 1), "When Israel out of Egypt came" (*MP* 2), "Half way, for one commandment broken" (*MP* 35), etc.

[37] Both of these couplets were written again on B 78.

PAGE 221, upper two thirds
Pencil, lightly erased in part; large X overscore.

And the youth at morning shine
  Makes the vow he will not keep.[38]

A sea too salt for drinking	And by whom made I know not,
But not too salt to drown.[39]	But 'twas not made for man.[40]

Then, in the hour when iron is sand
And mountains crumble, this should stand,
Nor falling firmament remove
The landmark of disastrous love.

The day the child comes to the birth
  He does not laugh, he cries:
So quick he learns the tune that earth
  Will sing him till he dies.

And from the bloody sea	And took the summer's tan

---

[38] This couplet is the genesis and the last two lines of "Westward on the high-hilled plains" (*ASL* 55), which occupies pages 20 and 21 of Notebook B.

[39] Possibly another foreshadowing of "The Oracles" (*LP* 25); cf. line 11: " 'Tis true there's better boose than brine, but he that drowns must drink it."

[40] Cf. *MP* 19, lines 5–6:

> Who made the world I cannot tell;
> 'Tis made, and here am I in hell.

Housman made but one entry (now lost) of this poem in the notebooks: on D 80–81, April 1922.

PAGE 231, lower two thirds

Pencil, much corrected and erased; beneath wavy cancellation in pencil.

The upper portion of the page contained the beginning of the unhappy romance of Nancy and Ned, whose story is continued on the surviving fragment. Whatever the preliminaries may have been, we may surmise

> How many hopes, how much desire
> Brought these two souls to the mire.

As for Nancy,

> Her father turned her from the door
> And she, like better folks before,
> She knew not where to lay her head.

She went at night in the rain to her lover's house, where Ned was sitting alone by a waning fire thinking of his sweetheart. "Long and speechless and apart" she stood outside the door while Ned stared into the graying embers. At length he was aroused

> When a foot came to the sill
> And a hand afraid to knock
> Fingered faintly at the lock.

"The rain blew in, the door swung wide," and Nancy weeping stood before her lover, who embraced her and wept with her. As they consoled each other, "in heaven the world-wide night" dropped its tears upon them.

PAGE 234, upper half
Pencil, beneath wavy cancellation in pencil.

Better to think your friend's unkind
  Than know your lover's untrue.

[   ]
  Oh man, the news will keep.
  Stay with the dead, man; stop your ears:
  There are worse things than sleep.[41]

  Oh Terence, Terence, the long way hither,
  The mist and the crying rain:
[   ]
  Must I go home again?[42]

---

[41] Cf. "To an Athlete Dying Young" (*ASL* 19), lines 15–16:

  And silence sounds no worse than cheers
  After earth has stopped the ears.

This poem was begun a short time after, on A 240.
  [42] The opening line of the first quatrain and the third of the second were not written.

PAGE 235, two sections; the middle third of the page missing
Pencil, lightly erased.

				starlight
"Hist, Terence, hist! wake up: 'tis I."[43]	[	?	] the moonlight fell
That was a voice I know.	[	?	] clear
Up I got and out I looked	To look at him you could not tell
And saw who stood below.	He had been dead a year.

The dead man in the moonless night
   Went back to find his grave.

---

[43] It is evident that these fragments and those on the preceding page are parts of the same poem. On the top portion of A 235, A. E. H. composed stanzas one and two and near the bottom of the page wrote the last two lines of the concluding stanza. The page opposite, number 234, was used for experimental sketching. Many verso-recto pages in the notebooks show this same division of labor: the recto page received the stanzas that were in the poet's mind as he opened his notebook; then turning back to the verso page he worked out the others.

PAGE 239, complete
Pencil, partly erased; much corrected.

Often, drinking, warm with ale,
Or laughing at an idle tale,
Into my heart the thought comes cold
How I forget my
Of my forgotten friends of old,
Lads that before light was gone
Put
Did the cap of darkness on.
What a clod of earth am I,
Forgetting fellows when they die.
[   ] any trifle glads
My heart, and you forgot, my lads.

Who could think that knew us then,
When you and I were living men,
And saw what friends we would seem
Who could think it, who could dream

And come to think [   ]
Poor fellows, I'm no worse than you;
 keep
I have you in mind no more,
But you forgot me long before.

'Twere strange if we alone should move
A mortal man to deathless love.

 Long it lasted, now
Cry you quits, then; there it ends,
I'll say no more that we were friends.[44]

---

[44] This poem, on an uncongenial theme, apparently was never taken up again in the notebooks. Its counterpart may be seen in "As through the wild green hills of Wyre" (*ASL* 37), which A. E. H. had opened on A 204 and was to resume on B 57. These lines, which echo some of those on A 239, are near the beginning of the draft on B 57:

 And "Don't forget us, lad," said they.
 Oh, I shall be stiff and cold
 When I forget you, hearts of gold:
 The country where I mind you not
 Is the land where all's forgot.

Date: April or May 1895

PAGE 12, complete
Pencil, beneath wavy cancellation in pencil; partly erased.

Wandered too long in the green shaws

[   ] now no more
Strip to bathe on Severn shore[1]

         honour is
In the land where all things are forgotten,
  In the company that kings' sons keep,
         all Kings
With the multitudes that never were begotten
    nation that shall never be begotten
  You shall sleep.

And you with colours gay
  And martial music swelling
Walk the resounding way
  To the still dwelling.[2]

[1] The second line of this imperfect couplet became number 6 of *ASL* 55. The first record of this poem appears on A 221 (*q.v.*), where Housman wrote (in January 1895 —about three months earlier) the two concluding lines of it. A few days after this entry in Notebook B he composed on pages 20 and 21 the four quatrains of the lyric.

[2] Cf. the last stanza of *LP* 7:

> And down the distance they
>   With dying note and swelling
> Walk the resounding way
>   To the still dwelling.

On B 176 (*q.v.*) a half-dozen years later, Housman wrote another line (number 16) of this poem, but did not take it seriously in hand until April 1922, when he was collecting the pieces that went into *Last Poems.*

'Tis because it thinks of nought
That the giddy world goes round[3]

Beer is good, and good are skittles,   'Tis the feather pate of folly
[   ] 'tis only thinking   Keeps the head from earth.
　　Lays lads underground.

　　the singing   head
'Tis a lightsome heart alone   'Tis the laughing heart alone
Sets   Keeps afoot the sullen bone
Drills to march the sullen bone   lie
　　That longs to lie in earth.   That longs to rot in earth.

　It is not
Is neither blood nor even tears

---

[3] In this and the remaining fragments on B 12 it is evident that Housman was commingling the stuff of two poems-to-be: *ASL* 43 and 49. Cf. *ASL* 43, lines 39, 40:

> And flesh and soul, now both are strong,
> Shall hale the sullen slaves along.

The entire poem should be read in this connection. Housman had made a nearly complete first draft of it on A 228–29 and rewrote it on B 72–73 in August 1895.
As to *ASL* 49, the complete poem should be quoted here:

> Think no more, lad; laugh, be jolly:
>   Why should men make haste to die?
> Empty heads and tongues a-talking
> Make the rough road easy walking,
> And the feather pate of folly
>   Bears the falling sky.
>
> Oh, 'tis jesting, dancing, drinking
>   Spins the heavy world around.
> If young hearts were not so clever,
> Oh, they would be young for ever:
> Think no more; 'tis only thinking
>   Lays lads underground.

　It was not until September or October 1895 (B 90) that Housman returned to the materials on the lower half of B 12 and composed the lyric that became *ASL* 49.

PAGE 42, upper two thirds
Pencil, lightly erased.

Streams of the forsaken west,[4]
Keep the hearts that I love best;
Keep your treasure, land and sea,
Shropshire breeds the men for me.
Golden lads and good to trust
Plant their heels in Shropshire dust;
On the western highways go
Lovely lads and good to know.

Corve and Teme and Severn shore,[5]
Countries where I come no more,
Under starlight now they stream
Broad along the lands of dream,
Only morning shows no more
Corve nor Teme nor Severn shore.

---

[4]Some minor substitutions in the manuscript of this poem have not been indicated.
[5]Cf. "As through the wild green hills of Wyre" (*ASL* 37), lines 27–28:

> And if my foot returns no more
> To Teme nor Corve nor Severn shore.

Housman began to work toward this draft of the couplet in his second attack on the poem (page 57 of Notebook B) one month later.

PAGE 44, upper half
Pencil, heavily erased.

[?   ] forgot
Lies in a land where I am not
And lays to sleep beyond the sea
The head that will not dream of me.[6]

---

[6] Above this quatrain the manuscript shows three or four illegible lines. The two stanzas here are an early essay at translating the Sapphic fragment that became *MP* 11, "The rainy Pleiads wester." The only other surviving notebook entry was copied on D 56, April 1922. An intermediate draft on B 225 has been destroyed.

Date: *July or August 1895*

PAGE 50, upper half
Pencil; some lines canceled and rewritten; not erased.

The Queen she sends to say[7]
That I must ride away:
Farewell, then,
So farewell, friends; my sovereign sends

And I must not say nay	And queens will take no nay
And queens will have their way	And what true man would stay?
	And treason 'twere to stay
She lends me a coach to ride	And no true man must stay[8]
With a man in blue outside.	
Such need of me, good soul, has she	
She will not be denied.	

Good bye, my lads, good bye;
There's no more tricks to try:

---

[7] Cf. "Grenadier" (*LP* 5), line 1: "The Queen she sent to look for me." Perhaps less than half of the poem on B 50 survives, but this portion of it foreshadows a jocular mood quite unlike that of the grim effect of "Grenadier."

[8] These lines (and the fifth in the left column) are tentative substitutes for line 4.

PAGE 55, middle half missing

Pencil, beneath wavy cancellation in pencil; partly erased.

glades
Strolling in the woods of Hay
Where once the Lady took her way
And the lighted palace stood
Midmost of the open wood.[9]

[   ] the floor is fallen, and there
pace
Maurice now must dance on air.[10]

[9] The romantic, faery-like tone of this quatrain is unique in the notebooks. It may also be noted that the words "palace" and "glade" are not found in Housman's *Collected Poems*.

[10] Cf. "On moonlit heath and lonesome bank" (*ASL* 9):

The dead man stood on air. (line 8)

And dead on air will stand
Heels that held up as straight a chap
As treads upon the land. (lines 22–24)

PAGE 66, lower two thirds
Pencil, slightly corrected; otherwise intact.

If your hand or foot offend you
    Cut it off, lad, and be whole;
But play the man, stand up and end you
    When your sickness is your soul.[11]

But I shall go and come no more
And two and two will still be four.[12]

They would not but they must

I would not but I shall

If it chance your
Sinner, if your eye offend you
      man, and
    Pluck it out, and so be sound;
      here are salves
'Twill hurt, but earth has balms to friend you
      balsam
And many a simple grows on ground.

[11] This quatrain and the one at the bottom afford an instructive view of Housman's manner of composition. The upper stanza (lacking only an introductory *And*) is the latter half of *ASL* 45. After writing it here, Housman toyed with the next four lines; then the theme of the quatrain forced itself upon him and he wrote the verses that eventually became stanza one of *ASL* 45, bringing them in this draft to the finality of printer's copy. It is evident that Housman prepared printer's copy from B 66, for no other version of *ASL* 45 ever existed in the notebooks.

[12] This fatalistic symbol Housman remembered and used in "When first my way to fair I took" (*LP* 35), line 9: "To think that two and two are four," written on B 160, c. 1900.

PAGE 78, complete
Pencil, beneath wavy cancellation in pencil.

And all between them, up and down,
  mere
By stream and hamlet, hill and town,
On many a belfry-shaded knoll[13]
Man has laid his mortal soul.

                              the kingdom-covering sky
                         All for me to walk upon
                              the heaven-edged hill

Hear the silent moon no more
Hale the starring seas ashore[14]

                              the blue-skied land
                         the world-wide fall of eve[15]
                              heaven-ascending
                         the heaven-upholding hills
                              far-beholding hill[16]
                    the unperished shade of night[17]

Here no hand on all the farm
Rouses at the false alarm[14]

[13] This line and others on this page show further examples of Housman's coinage of compound epithets. With "belfry-shaded" compare "steeple-shadowed" in *ASL* 61, line 15.

[14] These couplets had been written on A 220.

[15] It is probable that this phrase is an echo from "By shores and woods and steeples" (*MP* 38); cf. "The far-shed alms of eve" (line 4). The second (and nearly complete) draft of this poem was written on A 186 during the summer of 1894, antedating B 78 by nearly a year.

[16] The fact that this phrase had been inscribed on A 187 serves to establish further the connection of that area of Notebook A and B 78.

[17] Cf. "Her towering foolscap of eternal shade" (*LP* 36, line 8). This astronomical symbol was too good to be forgotten and on B 179, possibly five years later, A. E. H. wrote this couplet:

> Her vast and moon-eclipsing cone of night,
> Her towering foolscap of eternal shade.

On C 14 he wrote these two lines into their stanza, and on C 18 he composed stanzas three and one of the three-stanza poem, which was finally assembled on D 24 in the busy April of 1922.

And far below on field and glade
Trails the never-anchored shade.

'Tis not wonderful at all

Once he did from morn to night
Many things but nothing right.

Here I stand and I can see
Shropshire lying under me.

Move upon a mountained road.

PAGE 86, nearly complete; three sections
The upper two sections contain eight lines of the concluding portion of *ASL* 62. The lower section is in pencil, erased; beneath wavy cancellation in pencil.

[Because?]

Says the grenadier to me,
"Give me half-a-crown," says he.
To the grenadier says I,
"Very well, my lad, but why?"

"Why," says he, "for standing cheer
To a British grenadier."
So I put the money down
And he took my half-a-crown.

PAGE 93, complete

Pencil; slightly corrected; all but middle portion lightly scored with large X's.

       kind

If you'll be good to one another,

   That's the coin would pay me best;

But if man still must hate his brother,

   Hate away, lads, I will rest.

    2. The manful dead remain[18]

Oh on my breast in days hereafter

   Light the earth should lie,

Such weight to bear is now the air,

     seems

  So heavy is the sky.[19]

     hangs

[   ] against we die,

For some do say that die we shall

Scans the world for things to die for

Till the ice at her girdle shall meet from the south & the north

             quarrels

And man shall sit down from his labours and die of the cold.[20]

      That sees the [Maytime going],[21]

      Certain to die before it comes again

---

[18] The reason for the numeral is not clear. The line may have been intended as a substitute for one written earlier on a page that is now lost. Years later Housman wrote this line into an uncompleted quatrain on B 230 (*q.v.*).

[19] This quatrain was published as number 10 of *Additional Poems*.

[20] These lines were written into an uncompleted quatrain on C 5 (*q.v.*).

[21] The brackets are in the manuscript.

PAGE 101, complete

Pencil, corrected and lightly erased.

The seven entries on this page are a collection of alternatives, composed while the printer's copy of *A Shropshire Lad* was being prepared or after it had been sent off. All are tentative substitutes or additions to poems drafted in Notebooks A and B—some perhaps as far back as five years or more. The single brackets and the parentheses are in the manuscript.

The star from north and south returns[22]

Blows] Plays[23]

The wind] The gale (twice)[24]

Shot?] Today? Last night?[25]

hedge] fence[26]

Beneath the blue of day[27]

Gay the files of scarlet follow:[28]

[22] Cf. "1887" (*ASL* 1) line 3, "From north and south the sign returns." No draft of the stanza to which this line belongs has survived.

[23] This is a return to A 238, where Housman had written "Blows no wind of healing now"—line 14 of *ASL* 30, eventually printed "Plays no wind . . ." The early preference for *Blows* may have been a reminiscence from Matthew Arnold, "Lines Written by a Death-Bed," line 27.

[24] This is a correction for B 98, where Housman had drafted *ASL* 31 complete, writing two lines (3 and 21) beginning "The wind."

[25] On B 62 "Shot? so quick, so clean an ending?" was the opening line of the poem printed as *ASL* 44. The substitutes on B 101 were rejected.

[26] This refers to A 181 and the opening line of stanza two of *ASL* 36 drafted there: "Still hangs the hedge without a gust"—which was the line that survived to print.

[27] This line harks back to A 82, where Housman had written line 10 of *ASL* 14: "In all the ken of day," and later line-canceled it. The substitute here on B 101 was written into the proof sheet of the poem.

[28] This is the needed alternative to the vapid line which slipped into the first draft of the final stanza of *ASL* 35 on B 94: "These are feet and they can follow."

PAGE 139; one-inch strip from middle
Pencil; two lines slightly altered; unerased.

Planted deep on perished people,[30]

Chaps that sleep and never snore   My love, that I was born to die for

My love, for whom I cannot die[31]

My love, that I shall not be true to,
  Good bye, my love, good bye.

[29] The symbol (C) indicates a date supplied by Sir Sydney Cockerell. (See page 22 of this volume.)

[30] Possibly a recollection from A 144, where ten years earlier Housman had composed the first draft of "The farms of home lie lost in even" (*MP* 14); it concludes:

> There I was friends with perished people,
>   And there lie they.

Cf. also "The First of May" (*LP* 34) lines 19, 20:

> . . . where Ludlow tower
> Stands planted on the dead.

These lines were written first, probably, on B 153 (the page has been lost) and copied on B 171.

[31] Cf. the first and concluding lines of *AP* 20:

> I shall not die for you,
>
> . . . .
>
>   For I was luckless aye
> And shall not die for you.

There is no draft of this poem in the notebooks.

PAGE 147, complete
Pencil; every line canceled with two or three horizontal strokes in heavy pencil.

Spring will be [?] maying
 And winds [?]

[   ] fishermen of midnights
When the moon [?   ]

Shall sail the night [?]

The leagues of [?]

Oh, the flower springs of earth,
And whence it buds to birth
There it will travail long underground.

[   ] trumpets
 Blown in the empty night.

PAGE [159],[32] a one-and-one-fourth-inch strip cut from the middle
Pencil, beneath wavy cancellation in pencil; erased.

The checker-board of chance

---

[32] This page was not numbered, and the numeral which belonged to it was given
to the following page.

PAGE 159, upper two thirds
Pencil; the latter portions of the two lines beneath wavy cancellation in pencil.

> A certain time to joy and grieve
> And after that to rest.

PAGE 162, middle two thirds; two sections
Pencil, beneath wavy cancellation in pencil.

For man must kill or die

    The blue sky and the springing field[33]
        And high green hills I see

    Because out of the world he brings[34]
        And carries to the grave
    A head full of the thoughts of things
        He will not ever have.

---

[33] Cf. "Bredon Hill" (*ASL* 21), line 17: ". . . the springing thyme."

[34] This may have been at one time the fourth and concluding stanza of "When first my way to fair I took" (*LP* 35), which A. E. H. copied on page 160 of this notebook. This quatrain on B 162 completes the idea of the poem, which as printed lacks good sequence and falls short of finality. The use of the word *things* here may derive from ". . . things I could not buy" (line 4 of the printed version) and "To buy a thing . . ." (line 6).

PAGE 173, upper half
Pencil, much corrected and erased.

[   ] kernel
  [   ]
Nothing's eternal,
   My man, not even wrong.

        Soft are   notes
        Sweet is the flute
          And pleasant to the ears
       Of him that plays and even
         Of him that only hears.[35]

        Across the Shropshire brookside
        Along the clovered levels
          The western beam was laid.[36]

---

[35] This quatrain is a continuation of the first draft of "Fancy's Knell" (*LP* 41), which Housman had begun on B 172.

[36] These three lines are parts of the same draft, the second quatrain of the first stanza of the poem.

PAGE 176, middle third missing

Pencil, unerased; the page canceled with a long diagonal line beginning near the upper left corner.

fighter, nitre ∪ — ∪ — ∪ —
        ∪ — ∪ — ∪ — ∪
  ∪ — ∪ — ∪ —
    ∪ — ∪ — ∪   [37]

[   ] were they
  Nor clean of heart nor clever;
   for me
Only‸ they gave away[38]

               And both are sighing.[39]

[37] This table apparently contains the model on which these two lines were composed:

     Nŏr clēan ŏf hēart nŏr clēvĕr
     Ănd bōth ărĕ sīghĭng

[38] The page was cut through this line.

[39] This became line 16 of "In valleys green and still" (*LP* 7), only the last stanza of which Housman had written on B 12 during April or May 1895, perhaps seven years earlier. The first fifteen lines of the poem were not produced until April 1922—a few weeks before printer's copy for *Last Poems* was finished.

PAGE 180, middle third missing
Pencil, slightly corrected and erased.

And watch the grey-goose quill, the worse for drink,[40]
  Perform ancestral antics on the page
[   ] folk that cannot think
And yet delight to dip the pen in ink.

    No, they must lift their voice

    The thing they have not seen, no not in dreams

    Not one that knew his left hand from his right

---

[40] The lines on this page are improvisations on the satiric theme first exploited on A 220 (*q.v.*) and brought to a stage of completion on B 199.

PAGE 185, complete
Pencil, much corrected and heavily erased.

Now forms the line and faces
  The lead that spits and rains,
And fleet the red blood races
  Along the soldier's veins.

At all the gates it hammers
  And to heaven [sends a?] shout,
And shakes the bolts and clamours,
  "Ho, jailer, let me out."

It longs to smell the nitre[41]
  And play in sunshine warm
And paint the soldier brighter
  Than the Queen's uniform.

[41] It is of interest to note Housman's fondness for the word *nitre* and his efforts to work it into the rhyme of a stanza. Cf. B 176, where he had written *fighter, nitre*. The word does not appear in any of his hitherto published poems.

PAGE 194, complete
Pencil, beneath wavy cancellation in pencil.

Spring came to trespass in the winter field.

On me the morning glances,
To you the night is nigh.

'Tis gone tomorrow
But oh, 'tis here today.

fleets
And over streets and ports and towers
Pours the confounding night.[42]

the tilt of leaves

Since to the dead I journey
And these before me fare
[   ] the tourney
[   ] the lists of air [43]

[42] Cf. "Smooth between sea and land" (*MP* 45), the last line: "Pours the confounding main."

[43] This uncompleted quatrain may be an afterthought to "The Merry Guide" (*ASL* 42), finished in September 1890. Cf. the next-to-final stanza:

And midst the fluttering legion
Of all that ever died
I follow, and before us
Goes the delightful guide.

PAGE 204, complete

Pencil, beneath wavy cancellation in pencil; erased.

> Ay, kiss your girl and then forget her;[44]
>   'Tis like the brave:
> They love the leaden bullet better
>   To lie with in the grave.

[44] This quatrain has in it something of the seventh and ninth stanzas of "The Deserter" (*LP* 13). There is, however, no earlier draft of this poem in the notebooks and no later one other than the near-perfect version on D 41–42, from which printer's copy was taken. Thus it is evident that not all the intermediate drafts of the poems went into the notebooks.

Sir Sydney Cockerell writes (*London Times Literary Supplement,* 7 November 1936) that Housman said he began the poem in 1905 and finished it in April 1922; that it was "based on the tune of a chanty heard at Hereford."

PAGE 230, complete

Pencil, much corrected and erased. The upper half is covered with a draft (nearly illegible now) of "The Olive" (*AP* 23), which was fair-copied on the next page.

There are ten graves, and in the ten[45]
   The tale of dead is nine;
There in nine graves my countrymen,
   In my grave I am not.
   The empty grave is mine.

        the trade of
I too was taught to play the man,
   And read my lesson plain;
But they, when I forgot and ran,
   Remembered and remain.

The manful dead remain[46]
They caught and held the flying hour
  I shall not find again.   That never is again.

        lads   are under
There nine shrewd fellows stand their ground,
   The only fool was I,
To keep my carcass safe and sound
   And leave my name to die.[47]

[45] The lines on this page represent the first draft of "My dreams are of a field afar" (*MP* 39):

My dreams are of a field afar
   And blood and smoke and shot.
There in their graves my comrades are,
   In my grave I am not.

I too was taught the trade of man
   And spelt the lesson plain;
But they, when I forgot and ran,
   Remembered and remain.

The superscribed alternative for line 4 points the way taken by later revision—which had to wait perhaps nearly twenty years (D 14, lost).

[46] Cf. B 93, where this line was written about ten years earlier.

[47] In the printed version of the poem there is no trace of this stanza.

PAGE 3, upper half
Pencil, partly erased.

And then, a long time after,
  The [?   ] shall die[2]

                              Shires where the girls are fonder,[3]
                              Towns where the pots hold more.

        Niniveh
      Oh, Babylon
For where are Thebes and Sidon[4]
  And Troy, the Grecian town?
    once
They all were steepled cities,
  But oh, my lads, they're down.
And Ludlow's like to [?   ][5]

---

[1] Since only two of the surviving pages of Notebook C are dated by Sir Sydney Cockerell, it was thought advisable not to suggest dates in connection with the poems and fragments from C.

[2] Cf. "The First of May" (*LP* 34), lines 21–22:

> Our thoughts, a long while after,
> They think . . .

[3] This couplet is the first entry in the notebooks of "On forelands high in heaven" (*MP* 33) and became lines 11 and 12 of that poem. A. E. H. wrote perhaps a full draft of it on C 47–48 (only fragments of the pages remain) before writing fair copy on D 87–88.

[4] These four lines are further congelations of *MP* 33. Cf. lines 19–20:

> Troy was a steepled city,
> But Troy was far away.

[5] The page was cut through this line.

81

PAGE 5, complete

Pencil, beneath wavy cancellation in pencil.

[?   ] in circles the [?   ] she shall not behold
Till the ice at her girdle shall meet from the south and the north
And man shall sit down from his quarrels and die of the cold.[6]

---

[6] The last two lines of this unfinished quatrain Housman had written on B 93 at least five years earlier.

Page 118 of Notebook D: "Here, in the beechen forest"

PAGE 8, complete

Pencil, beneath wavy cancellation in pencil; overscored with a high up-and-down stroke.

Ned Lear and I were drunk last week,
　　Oh, dripping drunk were Ned and I,
Too drunk to see, too drunk to speak,
　　Too [　　　　　　　　　　　　]
You might have looked through Ludlow fair
And never spied a sillier pair.

To Ludlow fair the first of May
　　Two lovely lads, went I and Ned[7]

---

[7] These lines were copied from A 194 (*q.v.*) — copied by memory, it would seem, for Housman apparently did not turn back to his first notebook to get all of the fourth line.

Housman was recalling twenty lines written in a moment of inspiration at least six years previously, but he evidently liked the poem less the more he copied of it. There is a full half-page below the last line on C 8; but neither here nor later in the notebooks is there evidence that he took the poem in hand again.

PAGE 14, middle half missing

Pencil, corrected and partly line-canceled. The upper section of the page contains the second stanza of *LP* 36. The quatrain below is overscored with a rambling up-and-down line.

>   Cheer, for
> Rejoice: the time of tyranny is out,
>   heap
> The shards of Dagon strew the temple floor,
> Illuminated nations sing and shout.
> Let them; but heaven has heard that noise before.

PAGE 17, nearly complete; two sections, the upper one blank
Pencil, beneath wavy cancellation in pencil.

[   ] another soul

Hope and fear and hate and lust,[8]
  Foes and comrades, all are slain.[9]
Peace be with them, for I trust
  Never old or young again.

[8] Cf. "When I watch the living meet" (*ASL* 12), line 5: "If the heats of hate and lust," written on A 230 early in 1895.

[9] Cf. "Ask me no more, for fear I should reply" (*AP* 6), line 7: "And one was fond of me: and all are slain." The single notebook entry of the poem (B 124, early 1896) has been destroyed.

PAGE 18, complete

Pencil, beneath wavy cancellation in pencil. Stanzas one and two of *LP 36* occupy the lower two thirds of the page.

    Pity them not; they did not pity thee.

          [   ] the dead are fallen,
        I am alive and stand.[10]

---

  [10] These two lines are possibly a continuation of "My dreams are of a field afar" (*MP* 39), begun on B 230 (*q.v.*).

PAGE 21, complete
Pencil, beneath wavy cancellation in pencil.

It was too dark to see.

Though
When spring comes north and islands
    Turn leafy in the sea.[11]

[11] These two lines are the first omens in the notebooks of the interesting "Beech Tree" poem, composed twenty years or more later on D 118 (q.v.).

PAGE 28, complete

Pencil, beneath wavy cancellation in pencil.

[   ] the cold and turning tomb of man.

When skies at evening cloud[12]

    Not two or three or some
I will not [?   ]

Found one the friend I sought for,   Since men are born to toil,
    Lost is the shot I sped;   All, and not only some,
And every face I fought for   I will not outcry make
    Is old or dead.   Because my own is come.

                                 Whose troubles are to come[13]

Oh worse remains for others[14]
    And worse to fear had I   Not both the fight is for
Than here at five-and-twenty
    To lay me down and die.

The stars of heaven are steady,   (Mother, you bore a man.) [15]
    The founded hills remain,
Though I to dust and darkness
    Return in blood and pain.

Farewell, my mortal soul.

[12] Cf. the opening lines of *LP* 39:
           When summer's end is nighing
           And skies at evening cloud.

The line on C 28 is the first sign of the poem in the notebooks. Housman wrote a rough draft of it on C 90–91 (lost) and fair copy on D 27–28.

[13] This line is an alternative for the last line of the quatrain above.

[14] This quatrain and the following lines represent the first draft of *MP* 21, which was unsuccessfully resumed on D 31, 32, and 34, but brought to fair copy on D 119.

The first four lines of the poem on C 28 eventually became, with one word altered, the last of the four-stanza lyric. The second stanza here, with the change of a single word, became number two:

           The stars of heaven are steady,
           The founded hills remain,
           Though I to earth and darkness
           Return in blood and pain.

The line written at the bottom of the page was turned into the last line of stanza three: "Farewell, my aery soul."

[15] The signs of parenthesis are in the manuscript.

PAGE 42, upper half
Pencil; the first four lines intact, the remainder canceled with horizontal lines.

The old defenses abide[16]
And seaward returns the tide.
In surety that all stands fast
Lie down, defender, at last.

Lie down, defender, and sleep,
    Defender of Troy, sleep fast;
    Sleep fast, defender of old.
    While earth's foundations remain
            wake
  We shall not call you again.

[16] The first line begins in the extreme upper left of the page and suggests that the stanzas may have been the continuation of a poem begun on C 41 (lost).

PAGE 49, the middle half missing

Pencil. The writing on the upper section (shown below) is corrected and line-canceled; the lower section contains an intact draft of stanza two of *LP* 28.

      Unfriendly comes the dawn of light
      Dreary blooms at dawn the east [17]
          steals

Oh dreary
    Bitter is the morning's breath
          filmy
     Across the shivering pool,
         winter
   And shivering through the longest night
     The year goes out with Yule

[17] Housman canceled all but the first word of this line, struck out all of the next and the words *shivering* and *filmy* in the one following. This quatrain is his first approach to the opening stanza of *LP* 28, which he about twenty years later brought to the status of printer's copy on D 35:

    Now dreary dawns the eastern light
      fall of
   And ~~the ending~~ eve is drear,
    And cold the poor man lies at night,
    And so goes out the year.

On B 169 A. E. H. had composed a never-to-be-altered draft of what later became the second and concluding stanza of *LP* 28. On this page it followed the quatrain which was eventually published as *AP* 9: "When the bells justle in the tower." It is probable that these eight lines on B 169 were originally conceived as a single poem. Only a small portion of D 35 has survived—just enough to show the fair copy of stanza one—and we now possess no evidence that the two quatrains of *LP* 28 were ever actually written together in the notebooks.

Below the perfect stanza on B 169 there is the unfinished draft of another:

      [   ] to know
    Things I shall not ever do
      To the grave 'tis time to go.

NOTEBOOK D

Date: ?

PAGE 91, upper half
Faded ink, beneath wavy cancellation in heavy newer ink; overscored with an
X and a long rambling stroke.

> "Stand back, you men and horses,[1]
>   You armies, turn and fly;
> You rivers, change your courses
>   And climb the hills, or I
>   Will know the reason why.
>
> "Die above, O tempests brewing,
>   I will have heaven serene;
> Despair, O tides, of doing
>   The mischief that you mean,
>   For I will stand between.
>
> "Death, turn your dart and blunt it,
>   Hell, take and break your bow[2]

---

[1] This poem is reminiscent of some of Housman's *juvenilia* which his brother published in *My Brother, A. E. Housman,* pp. 30–38. (See also William White's publication of "Sir Walter Raleigh" in *Etudes Anglaises,* vol. 6, no. 4 (November 1953), pp. 346–49; and his reprint of "The Death of Socrates" in *PMLA,* vol. 68, no. 4, part 1 (September 1953), pp. 913–16. The first poem was written when A. E. H. was 14; the second a year later.) Certainly the Olympian air of the poem on D 91 is not found elsewhere in the notebooks. The faded ink and the heavy later canceling of this page compare with the appearance of some of the opening pages of Notebook A.

[2] The page was cut through this line; the poem was continued on D 92 (lost).

PAGE 113, complete

Faded ink, beneath wavy cancellation in heavy newer ink.

> From the brief and [winter?] day[3]
> And its little [   ] of light,
> I shall take to bed away
> Things to dream of all the night.

[3] These four lines were written on the verso side of the sheet that contained the poem "For My Funeral" (*MP* 47), which was headed by the date "Jan. 1925." It may be that the quatrain reiterates symbolically some of the ideas of *MP* 47.

It was on D 110 or 111 that A. E. H. made the first entry in that notebook after completing printer's copy for his second volume in mid-June of 1922.

PAGE 116, upper half
Pencil, intact.

I dreamt I was reading a passage of George Eliot, in which was quoted, printed in italics as prose, the verse[4]

> The bogle of the [hairy weid]*[5]
> That beast nor man hath trod
> Must not be seen of you nor me
> Nor aught but hell and God.
>
> *understood as a heath or moor[4]

[4] These are the only prose notes surviving in the notebooks.
[5] The brackets and the note are in the manuscript.

PAGE 118, complete

Faded ink, beneath wavy cancellation in heavy newer ink; corrections and alternative stanzas in pencil, erased.

Here, in the beechen forest,
    When spring and love were new,
I took my knife last April
    And carved the names of two.

I sealed for years and ages
    What lived a briefer day:
Lost is the letters' meaning,
    The tablet shall not stay.

What lived a little day
        worn away
What months have seen decay[6]

Still, though the sense is perished,
    Letter and tablet stay.[6]

So here I bring the auger
    And in the hole I drill
I pour out all the evil,
    The vitriol sure to kill.

        May
Next year in our green woodland
    Shall stand a naked tree,
Where spring comes north and islands
    Turn leafy in the sea.[7]

I sealed for years and ages
    What months have spilt and shed;
Lost is the letters' meaning,
    The tablet yet is read.

October comes and carries
    Life with the leaves
    Eternal things away;

Eternal things are perished,
The sense has left the tablet.

    Their tablet shall not stay.

[6] These lines and the two quatrains at the bottom of the page represent efforts at reconstructing the second stanza.

[7] This poem, in spite of the corrections surrounding it, appears to have been left by the poet in nearly the same "read and approved" status as four others in the latter dozen pages of Notebook D. The heavy ink cancellation is obviously much later than the date of the draft of the poem. There is no X in the upper right corner—the sign of a poem's inferiority, which may be seen for example on the page opposite, where Housman wrote an uncorrected copy of the lyric later printed as *MP* 37.

It is a safe presumption that "Here, in the beechen forest" belongs with the poet's sanctioned output. It actually is the ultimate product of his poetic fancy, for the remainder of Notebook D was (with the exception of six pages of humorous verse) taken up with redrafts of older pieces. The lyric on D 118 is A. E. Housman's last poem.

PART THREE

Abandoned Lines and Stanzas in the
Notebooks and Foolscap Sheets

THE early drafts of a large number of the pieces contained in Housman's *Collected Poems* include stanzas, couplets, and single lines that were replaced by alternatives or abandoned altogether. Some of these passages were evidently canceled immediately after they were written, and their substitutes set over them before the next lines were composed; others seem to have been thrown out in a line-by-line review of the poem, perhaps many years after it was first set down; and still others passed unscathed into second, third, or fourth drafts and were replaced only in a final notebook copy or in the copy that went to the printer.

The record of cancellation and erasure clearly shows, sometimes amusingly, Housman's states of mind in the pale cast of revision, which, if we may generalize from his remarks in his Leslie Stephen lecture, was a laborious process.[1] The inept, faltering phrase thrown down in the haste of composition he savagely annihilated with the eraser or drowned in meandering ink. Sometimes, as if he feared by weighing one word at a time he might let another, the right one, escape forever, he desperately sprinkled beneath a gaping line a half-dozen substitutes or more. Thus for the beginning of the fourth line of "The Lent Lily" (*ASL* 29) A. E. H. wrote *Bejewelling, Emblazoning, Illumining, Embroidering, Enamelling, Bedizening, Apparelling*—and rejected them all.

---

[1] *The Name and Nature of Poetry,* pp. 49–50.

Rose Harland of "This time of year a twelvemonth past" (*ASL* 25) was once Jane Crossley, then Rose Archer, again Rose Andrews. There are comparatively few proper names in the early drafts of the notebooks that went on into print unchallenged. The lads in their hundreds at one time came into *Wenlock* for the fair, not into *Ludlow* (*ASL* 23); it dawned not in *Asia* but at *Cabul* and in *India* (*ASL* 1); Severn ran down to *Bewdley*, not *Buildwas* (*ASL* 28).

Though it is obvious that Housman expressed his disgust in striking out some of the passages collected in the pages that follow here, there must have been a few that he abandoned more in sorrow than in anger. One of these will not suffer by comparison with the quatrain that replaced it in *MP* 15:

> Tarry, delight; we seldom meet.
> Day peeps not yet, though soon it will.
> A star or two has still to fleet
> Beyond the western hill. (D 52)

Some of the rejected lines—for example, the unused stanza of " 'Farewell to barn and stack and tree' " (*ASL* 8, see page 99)— would have made significant changes in narrative; others would have deepened or lightened the mood of a lyric, pointed the satire, suggested a personal testimony, or repeated a well-loved name. All are interesting for what they reveal of the development of the poems of which they were once a part.

THE NOTEBOOKS

A 113 "I wake from dreams . . ." (*MP* 43) first draft:
Unlocated stanza

> What world-appalling message
> Illegible and high
> Is yon that [showeth?] presage
> The gazer of the sky?

A 133 "Bredon Hill" (*ASL* 21) first draft:
Lines 21, 22

> But on a winter morning
> When all the roads were stone,

Abandoned Lines and Stanzas

Opening lines of stanza 6

        All
There in the tower hung silent
   The chime I thought would be;

     tolled
They rang but one bell only
   For more there might not be:

       chimes
The wedding peals were silent
   That will not ever be;

They tolled but one bell only,
   And so, *etc.*[2]

A 136–37 "The Sage to the Young Man" (*MP* 4) second draft:

Abandoned second stanza

     bearest   braver
Who art stayed on surer trust
   Than fear or sloth shall quell,
And under heel hast thrust
   The threats of hungering hell:

Stanza to follow number 5

The loser hath not less,
   They have not more that win:
One wage for righteousness
   And one like wage for sin.

Following the stanza just quoted

To no man's hand for aye
   Is given to keep the prize:
Content thee if today
   Thou see it with thine eyes.

A 143 "Bredon Hill" (*ASL* 21) second draft:

Line 27

And silent were the three,

No wedding chimes had we,

And few came out to see,

And groom was none to see,

[2] The remainder of the manuscript here is the same as the printed text.

A 145 "From far, from eve and morning" (*ASL* 32) second draft:
Lines 9, 10

> How would you have me help you
> Unlock
> Show me your soul and say,

A 147 "Be still, my soul, be still . . ." (*ASL* 48) first draft:
Lines 1–3

> no help will come of
> no profit is in hating
> will not mend with grieving
>
> Be still, my soul, be still, it never can be mended:
> This heaven and earth were fixt of old and founded strong.
> Be still and call to thought to while the hour of waiting
> Think and recall to mind to speed the while of waiting
> The days, *etc.*

A 165 "If truth in hearts that perish" (*ASL* 33) second draft:
Lines 9, 10

> Hot hope   contriving
> Long care and vain devising
>
>   pains
> And hopeless toil to please,—
>
> Fear and hot hope and thinking
> Long fear and hope and striving
>
> And sick despair to please

A 170 "March" (*ASL* 10) the unique draft:
Stanza 2

> So now of nights the storm-cock sings
> To move the rusted wheel of things,
> And trout in brook and herd on plain
> And beasts are glad on all the plain
> Leap that   es
> To feel the world go   round again.

A 175 "Stars, I have seen them fall" (*MP* 7) the unique draft:
Lines 5, 6

> The thing that was will be,
> Naught helps the primal fault;

Abandoned Lines and Stanzas

A 191 "'Farewell to barn and stack and tree'" (*ASL* 8) the unique draft:

Title, Severn Shore

Stanza to follow number 3

> Let Lucy sorrow that she was born
>> To set us two to strive:
> If she loves the lad she loved at morn
>> She loves no lad alive.

Line 15

> At home I've no more work to make,
>
> Today an end of work we make,
>
> For no more work at home we make,
>
> We've sweat our last on scythe and rake,

A 192 "The Isle of Portland" (*ASL* 59) the unique draft:
Lines 1–3

> The wind at sea from France tonight
>> Is soft to England blown;
> High juts behind the Portland light

A 193 "Hughley Steeple" (*ASL* 61) the unique draft:
Lines 21–24

> ne'er
> scarce
> 'Twill not be lonesome, truly,
>> sleep with friends
>> To lie by lads one knows,
> tower
> When underground at Hughley
>> rest   by
>> I sleep with these or those.

A 209 "In midnights of November" (*LP* 19) first draft:
Stanza 1

> In winds at midnight plying
>> timber
>> The leafless poplar roars;
> And the dead call the
> The dead call to the dying
>> finger
>> And whistle at the doors.

Abandoned second stanza

> I hear my comrades hollo,
>> friends
>> Too long we lads are twinned,
>> Oh
> And I will rise and follow
> Along the snowy wind

A 211 "The True Lover" (*ASL* 53) second draft:
Stanza 1

> He whistled soft and out of sight
> In shadow of the boughs.
> "Come down, my girl, for now is night,
> And lovers crown their vows."

Abandoned second stanza

>>> his
>> She rose, she followed at the call,
>> And
>> She knew not why nor how.
>>> boy
>> "I never loved the man at all:
>> What takes me to him now?"

Final stanza

> Beyond the tree the moon made light,
> But none beneath the boughs,
> And all was in the whispering night,
> When lovers crown their vows.

A 214 "R. L. S." (*AP* 22) first draft:
Lines 5–7

> Home is the hunter from the hill;
>> Haled
>> And in the heaven-wide snare,
> The brutes lie captives of his skill

Lines 9–11

> But still's the foot that nought could flee,
>> steering hand
>> The hand that steered is still,
> And home the sailor from the sea,

Abandoned Lines and Stanzas

A 218 "Reveille" (*ASL* 4) first draft:
Stanza 1

> Yonder round the world returning
> Slow the tide of twilight spills
> And the ship of sunrise burning
>   beyond
> Heaves behind the eastern hills.
> Strands upon

Lines 13, 14

>   Towns and counties
> Land and cloudland woo together,
>   Hill-tops beacon
> Hills send signal, countries call:
> Ne'er a lad, *etc.*

A 219 Same poem, second draft:
Line 21

>   Feet   wrought
> Legs   Lads were born to play the rover,
>
> Rest for night, a lad's a rover;
>
>   Dust lies
> Stones lie still but blood's a rover;

A 222 "The Recruit" (*ASL* 3) second draft:
Titles, 'Listing; The Queen's Shilling
Line 3

> And luck to soldiers marching

Line 15

>   leave
> Lads you knew will like you

A 223 Same poem, third draft:
Unlocated lines and stanzas

> And luck to all your marching
> And here's good luck from Ludlow
> And keep your friends in mind, lad
>
> And if till doomsday thunder
> In lands of morn you lie,
>
> Ears that heard you speaking

And hands that held your hand
Will keep the thought to friend them
While Ludlow tower shall stand.

And you your head till doomsday
On lands of morn may lay
And make the lads of Ludlow
Unhappy
Wild sorrow far away.

A 227 "On moonlit heath and lonesome bank" (*ASL* 9) second draft:
Stanza 5

And helpless to the hangman's noose
In blue of morn will go
liefer die to loose
A neck I'd keep for kinder use
string it up for
Than break it for a show.

Stanza 6

And quick to nine the minutes post,
When still on air will stand
In shoes I'd liefer black than most
That walk upon the land.

Last line of an abandoned stanza

Strike eight, and soul and flesh will part.

A 229 "The Immortal Part" (*ASL* 43) first draft:
Stanza 1

Eve and morning, every day
I hear my bones within me say
'Another eve, another morn,
It is long till we be born.'

Lines 5, 6

When shall this slough of flesh be cast,
This tyranny be overpast

B 7 "As I gird on for fighting" (*LP* 2) the unique draft:
Stanza 1

As I tie on for battle
My sword upon my thigh
I think what may have happened
other
To better men than I.

102

Abandoned Lines and Stanzas

B 10 "To an Athlete Dying Young" (*ASL* 19) second draft:
Lines 11, 12

> And glory for the runner braids
> A chaplet briefer than a maid's.

Lines 17, 18

> No fear you now should join the throng
>   stayed   spell
> Of lads that lived a day too long,

B 14 "This time of year a twelvemonth past" (*ASL* 25) first draft:
Stanza 1

>   'tis a twelvemonth past,
> Ted Harland, fourteen months ago
>   When he and I would meet
> Would start some quarrel, till at last
> To settle which should walk with Jane
>   We fought and I was beat.

B 15 Same poem, second draft:
Stanza 4

> He keeps his bed now days are warm,
>   And clay's the bed he keeps;
> When Rose and I walk arm in arm
>   Fred Loughton lies and sleeps.

B 28 "He looked at me with eyes I thought" (*MP* 41) the unique draft:
Final stanza

>   stepped stood stept out
> Once he [?   ] but now my friend
>   marching
> Is not in walking trim,
>   march
> And you must tramp to the world's end
>   To touch your cap to him.

B 34 "Loveliest of trees, the cherry now" (*ASL* 2) first draft:
Stanza 2

> And since my days are days of men,
> And only threescore years and ten,
> And take from seventy springs a score
> It only leaves me fifty more,

103

And since of threescore years and ten,
Twenty will not come again,
And yet, of all the springs in store,
I shall see but fifty more.

B 35 "From the wash the laundress sends" (*MP* 29) the unique draft:
Couplet to follow line 4

Sized and starched without a speck,
And fit them round a Shropshire neck.

Line 5

Shropshire linen, Shropshire hearts,

B 39 "It is no gift I tender" (*AP* 4) the unique draft:
Stanza 1

It is no gift I offer
    A loan is all I may,
But take you yet the proffer,
    Though 'tis not made for aye.

B 46 "It nods and curtseys and recovers" (*ASL* 16) the unique draft:
Line 7

                                     a
There are worse sleepers than the lover

Not even love disturbs the lover

The lad that sighs is not the lover

Sleep has enamoured so the lover

The lad to sigh is not the lover

No longer sighing is the lover

B 53 "The Carpenter's Son" (*ASL* 47) first draft:
Unlocated couplet

Lock your heart and sink the key
With the millstone in the sea

Lines 19, 20

They the fruit of stealing prove—
Here the midmost hangs for love.

Abandoned Lines and Stanzas

B 57 "As through the wild green hills of Wyre" (*ASL* 37) second draft:
Unlocated lines

> And sure, the way's not hard to find:
> I need but bear my friends in mind.

> Pen the fold and mind the till

> Ludlow
> By Teme and Ony, Corve and Clee,

B 58 "The winds out of the west land blow" (*ASL* 38) second draft:
Last two lines of an uncompleted stanza

> So far the east is from the west
> The wind has lost the word.

B 62–63 "Shot? so quick, so clean an ending?" (*ASL* 44) second draft:
Lines 1, 2

> Nineteen! so quick and clean an ending?
> Oh you did right, lad, you were brave:

Lines 13, 14

> Before the noon
> Before 'twas high you guessed the morrow
> And took the ruinous end on trust.

> You would not brook the fate-fouled morrow
> wade   mud
> Nor tread the leagues of mire you must.

Another variant of the same, B 64, third draft

> clouding
> sullying ruinous
> You would not breast the blackening morrow
> Nor do and bear the wrong you must.

B 67 "Reveille" (*ASL* 4) third draft of second stanza only:
Lines 5, 6

> Wake; the axe[3] of morning shatters
> Shadows through [   ]

> Wake; the roof of shadow shatters
> Splintered on the plain it spanned,

> broken
> Wake; the breaking shadow scatters
> Splinters on the plain it spanned

[3] Here *axe* means "axis."

B 69 " 'Is my team ploughing' " (*ASL* 27) second draft:
Lines 19, 20

> And has she ceased from crying
> At to-fall of the eve?

> And has she ceased her crying
> When she lies down at eve?

B 72–73 "The Immortal Part" (*ASL* 43) second draft:
Lines 1, 2

> When at morn I heave my head
> Or lay me down at eve to bed,

Lines 7, 8

>   web
> This fluttering veil of life be torn
> And you be dead and we be born?

Lines 33, 34

> Flesh and soul are garments cast;
> The bone that wore them long shall last.

B 75 "When smoke stood up from Ludlow" (*ASL* 7) the unique draft:
Stanza 1

> As blithe afield to labour
>   Through dewy lanes asteam
> I strode beside the waggon
>   Against the morning beam
>   And whistled to the team,

Stanza 5

> Then my soul within me
>   Kept up the echo long,
> And still beside my horses
>   It sang the blackbird's song
>   The dewy lanes along.

> Then in my heart the echo
>   Took up the blackbird's strain
> [And still beside my horses][4]

[4] This line was not copied here in the manuscript.

steamy
Along the dewy lane
tune
It sang the song again.

B 85–86 " 'Terence, this is stupid stuff' " (*ASL* 62) second draft:
Line 56

Against you tread where I have trod;

Line 66

He tasted all that Asia bore;

B 87–88 Same poem, third draft:
Line 5

[   ] the pains you poets take

But meant 'twas not, and no mistake

Abandoned lines

How well his vaccination took,—

I think these bits of vine I glean
If you come where I have been
May be good for heart and head[5]

B 89 "When the lad for longing sighs" (*ASL* 6) the unique draft:
Stanza 1

starving
When the pleading lover sighs,
   When his looks are wan and pale,
When the lad looks nigh to death,
   Maiden, *etc.*

Line 3

Though at point of death
When against death's door he lies,

Stanza 3, in part

You can buy them: eve and morn:
   heal him
Cheap enough a maid can buy
   What the lover longs to sell
You can lay you down and die[6]

[5] Cf. line 56, "It should do good to heart and head."
[6] The page was cut below this line.

B 90 "Think no more, lad; laugh, be jolly" (*ASL* 49) second draft:
Lines 9, 10

> If young fellows would be gay
> Oh, they would be young for aye

B 92 "Say, lad, have you things to do?" (*ASL* 24) the unique draft:
Lines 2, 3

> Do them quick while life's at prime:
> What's a friend for? buckle to:

Lines 6, 7

> while I hear you
> Call me, I shall come at call;
> Wait not till they lay me low

B 95 "In midnights of November" (*LP* 19) second draft:
Line 1

> The brim of Severn freezes

Stanza 4

> I hear my comrades hollo,
>   And friend from friend is twinned,
> And I will rise and follow
>   Along the rainy wind.

B 99 "The lads in their hundreds . . ." (*ASL* 23) first draft:
Lines 1–3

> The lads from the country to Wenlock come in for the fair,
>   pleasant
>   And there are the welcome to hear and the good to behold,
>   ready to help and the safe to believe in
> The steady to trust and the ready to help you are there,

Lines 13–15

>   know
> But no, they have nothing to tell them by
>   the streets through the midst of us,
>   As crossing unknown through the market place, not to be told,
>   safety
> They carry unspoilt into darkness the honour of man,

Abandoned Lines and Stanzas

B 100 Same poem, second draft:
Line 2

smart

And there are the straight and the sprack and the good to behold,

Line 5

       town   farm   till

They come from the fold and the grange and the plough and the cart,

Line 9

I wish they were sealed on their foreheads; there should have been tokens to tell

Line 12

And bring them a mile on the way that they will not return.

Line 13

But now you can never be sure of them, try as you can;

B 160 "When first my way to fair I took" (*LP 35*) second draft:
Stanza 2

> There's less I'd care to choose today,
>   But what I would I can;
> The pence are here, and nought's away
>   Except the dead young man.

B 161 Same poem, second stanza only

> Today is altered: what I care
>   To buy myself I can;
> The pence are here, and so's the fair,
>   But not the dead young man.

B 169 Probably intended for "Now dreary dawns the eastern light" (*LP* 28):
An uncompleted stanza, to follow the second stanza

> [   ] to know
> Things I shall not ever do
>   To the grave 'tis time to go.

B 172 "Fancy's Knell" (*LP* 41) first draft:
Uncompleted quatrain for stanza 1

> [   ] and level
>   The beam from Wales was laid,
> And to the revel
>   I fetched my pipe and played.

B 182 "The West" (*LP* 1) second draft:
An uncompleted quatrain following stanza 8

> No need at all to look and lose
> Your heart upon the ebb of hues[7]
> 'Tis all too soon your [   ]

A line for stanza 8

> Stand and stem the ebb of hues[7]

B 184 Same poem, third draft:
A couplet for stanza 8

> And lovers lose their heads and lose
> Their hearts upon the ebb of hues

B 191 "Illic Jacet" (*LP* 4) second draft:
Abandoned opening lines

> Oh, girls are in love with their lovers,
>   But lads are in love with the grave

Stanza 1

> Oh hard is the bed that you cumber
>   But still 'tis the bed for the brave.
> No mattress to match it for slumber
> It has not its fellow for slumber
>   When lads are in love with the grave.

Opening lines of last stanza

>   quilt
> Oh thin is the sand but it covers
>   A heart that has found its repose,

[7] Cf. "Outward in the ebb of hues . . ." *MP* 46, line 10.

Abandoned Lines and Stanzas

B 195 "Grenadier" (*LP* 5) the unique draft:
Line 13

> And oh to strike the bargain twice!
> must take
> And I shall fetch a lower price

B 203 "The Oracles" (*LP* 25) the unique draft:
Line 14

> *Three hundred to the miles of men that reach from here to there;*

B 219 "Fancy's Knell" (*LP* 41) third draft:
Second quatrain of stanza 1

> Where on
> Across the brookside levels
>   The lowshot beam was laid,
>   To speed
> And to the revels
>   I fetched, *etc.*

First three lines of same

>   western
>   And where the low sun's lances
> Where low the sunsped lances
>   Along the mead
> On sward and bank were laid,
> On mead and stream
>   time
> To speed the dances

Opening lines of stanza 2

>   are tunes at
> Blithe at fall of even
>   And well; they please
> Is music in the ears
> Of him that plays, and even
>   Of him that only hears;
>   when tunes are
> And blithe, with music playing,
>   To watch on tree and steep
> The light, *etc.*

Stanza 2

> Ours were idle pleasures
> > Yet well content we were,
> > The rest to tread
> From him that trod the measures
> > And I to play the air
> > To him that played the air.
> To play the air, and playing
> > From tree & tower
> > To watch on tree & steep
> The light delaying, *etc.*

B 221 "Astronomy" (*LP* 17) the unique draft:
Title, The Use of the Globes
Line 7

> He hove the Southern Cross and sank

B 230 "The Olive" (*AP* 23) first draft:
Lines 2, 3

> > iron   trench fence
> > If steel could plant it sure
> > lead
> > And blood could [   ]

> > If man could fence it sure
> > From blights and blasting mildew
> > And fire could [   ] the mildew

Line 5

> > Shading the bloody trenches
> > If blood could rich the trenches

C 29 "Spring Morning" (*LP* 16) second draft:
Line 6

> > Wrung
> > Stiff with winter aches and pains

Lines 9, 10

> > Well the pleasurable air
> > With the turning earth runs on;

C 31–32 "The Land of Biscay" (*MP* 46) second draft:
Lines 3, 4

At the utmost bourn of journeys, the last step that ocean stays,
Once at eve we old companions, grief and I, we came to gaze.

Abandoned Lines and Stanzas

Where the earth across the ocean looks at nothing but the sky
On the far-beholding, *etc.*

Line 10

                    shade of earth
Sunward   shut of eve   land's
Outward from the fall of night, the dusking earth's unhappy pale

Line 13

          vessel
Now the pinnace neared the foreland, now the gazer, *etc.*

On she came and right for landing, till, *etc.*

Line 15

              amber
Now you saw the silver bulwark, round the prow you read her name

Line 17

              sunshine
From his ship of gold and silver he was, *etc.*
                amber
                sunfire

C 98 "Eight O'Clock" (*LP* 15) second draft:

Lines 3, 4

          One, two, three, four, on jail and square and people
              They dingled down.

D 19 "Epithalamium" (*LP* 24) second draft:

Opening lines

              Hie you hither, day is done,
              Hymen out of Helicon.
              Now to bower the bride is gone
                    lover
              Happy bridegroom, light of heart,
              Hail the god that joins to part.
              Here the groomsman shall abide
              While the bridegroom, *etc.*

                                    ripe
              Youth accomplished, manhood come

Lines to follow number 26

              Full
              High and steady, not to tilt,
              Safe, unsullied, nothing spilt

D 26 Prologue poem to *More Poems,* second draft:
Line 2

> For he that spells it scans

Line 5

> unlucky
> I make it for unhappy fellows

D 27 "When summer's end is nighing" (*LP* 39) third draft:
Lines 6, 7

> The gusts abroad at sunset
> Would ride the tilted ray,

D 31 "The world goes none the lamer" (*MP* 21) second draft
Lines 9, 10

> And so farewell my kingdom   fortunes
> That I could not control;

D 34 Same poem, the same lines:

> possessions
> Good-bye to all that ever   the havings
> I had or earned or stole;

D 38 "The rain, it streams on stone and hillock" (*LP* 18) third draft:
Lines 7–10 (stanza 2)

> Not you nor I, for sure.
> Man and remembrance, both decay,
> The loving-kindness like the day,
>   Not even ills endure
> And nothing can endure.

Lines 16–20 (originally stanza 3)

> The rain, it is not always raining,
>   Nor man the grave beside.
> Time and again shall I be glad,
>   chance on
> And find me friends like you, my lad,
>   The world it is so wide.

Lines 18–19

> delight
> I shall be blithe in morning's blue,
> Be gay with friends as good as you,
>   Or why's the world so wide?

Abandoned Lines and Stanzas

D 45 "The chestnut casts his flambeaux . . ." (*LP* 9) third draft:
Stanza 3

> And, I suppose, we two are not the first
>> That sat in taverns when the tempest hurled
> Their plans awry, and drank good ale, and cursed
>> Whatever sturdy blackguard, *etc.*

D 49 Same poem, fourth draft:
Line 19

> handful Our sorry portion is the estate of man
A sorry bundle are the rights of man:

D 51–52 "Tarry, delight, so seldom met" (*MP* 15) second draft:
Lines 3, 4

> [   ] and late we met
>> And soon shall part for long.

Stanza 1

>> Last on   and fail not yet
> Tarry, delight; we seldom meet,
>> Day peeps not yet, though soon it will.
>> train of stars
> A star or two has still to fleet
>> Beyond the western hill.

D 53 "In valleys green and still" (*LP* 7) third draft:
Lines 17–19

>> ever onward
> And deep in distance they,
>> The quickstep faintly swelling,
> Pace the resounding way

D 57 "Epithalamium" (*LP* 24) third draft:
Lines to follow number 26

>> Steadied truly not to tilt,
> Never shook nor turned atilt,
>> Carried far and nothing spilt.

D 60 Same poem, fourth draft:
Line 3

>> Conquering   stedfast
> Happy lover, constant heart,

115

D 69–71 "Hell Gate" (*LP* 31) first draft:
Lines 53, 54

> Back and forward
> Only sparkled as he crossed
> By the lintel
> The shut doorway of the lost.

Line 66

> And amidmost of the gate

> And before the guarded gate

Lines 68, 69

> While
> And the city far within
> Sounded with a busy hum

To follow line 98

> And about him as he strode,
> While   murk and blinded
> And the ever-mounting road
>   still-ascending
> [Wound along?] and brought us higher,
> Failed the, *etc.*

D 84 "In midnights of November" (*LP* 19) third draft:
Lines 3, 4

>   shipwreck seamen
> And storms that seamen drown for
>   Are angry in the sky.

D 86 "The half-moon westers low, my love" (*LP* 26) first draft:
Line 1

> The moon is lost at sea, my love,

Line 7

>   love
> And 'tis all one to you, my dear,

D 107 "The rain, it streams on stone and hillock" (*LP* 18) fifth draft:
Line 12

> To many a country wide:

Line 17

> The skies
> And heaven will yet be blue;

Abandoned Lines and Stanzas

Unlocated line

> Nor sorrow springing new;

D 121 "Young is the blood that yonder" (*MP* 34) second draft:
Line 21

> 'tis like
> Yet backs, I think, have burdens

Line 23

> As fell to flesh its portion
>
> [   ] had thoughts to plague it

THE FOOLSCAP SHEETS, L.C. VOLUME VI

L.C. 134 "On forelands high in heaven" (*MP* 33):
Line 10

> The gold and amber shore;

L.C. 137 "Smooth between sea and land" (*MP* 45):
Line 4

> Man born of
> The seed of woman plays.

Lines 24, 25

> Niniveh built to last
>   scored
> And *Sappho* scrawled in vain
> And scrolls inscribed in vain,
>   letters scored

L.C. 141 "Easter Hymn" (*MP* 1):
Line 4

> Smokes to the firmament and fires the night

L.C. 143 "Delight it is in youth and May" (*MP* 18):
Lines 10, 11

> And after dark the nightingale
> Begins beneath the hill.

L.C. 144 "Good creatures, do you love your lives" (*MP* 26):
Title, I counsel you beware

L.C. 145 "In midnights of November" (*LP* 19) :
Line 1

        When Martinmas is over,

Lines 3, 4

        And storms that drown Orion   the seaman
        Are angry in the sky,

Line 5

        About the bed I sleep in

        About the loosened chimneys

L.C. 147 "The Culprit" (*LP* 14) :
Title, The only son
Lines 12, 13

        Below the turf they lie:
        They do not ask their wages,
        They did not wait for pay-day,
                take their wages,

Stanza to follow number 3

        My mother and my father,
         I curse you, fool and knave,
        That bore me for the gallows,
         And got me for the grave,
         And would not save.

Lines 21, 22

        Farewell, good folk and evil;
        To-day the tale is done.

L.C. 148 "As I gird on for fighting" (*LP* 2) :
Unlocated stanza

              thirst   hunger
        I think on wounds and [marching?]
         And leaguers none relieve
        And routs and standards taken
         In battles lost at eve.[8]

[8] Cf. "In the battle lost at eve" (*AP* 2, line 8).

Abandoned Lines and Stanzas

L.C. 149 "Sinner's Rue" (*LP* 30):

Subtitle, after Heine [9]

Line 7

> And so the flower of azure

Lines 13, 14

> In the low herb was healing
> solace
> And courage in the sign,

> I plucked a herb of saining
> In the frail leaf is saining
> And comfort in the sign,

> That was   saining
> I plucked a herb of healing,
> A solace and a sign

Unlocated lines

> [   ] the night-jar only
> Spoke from the midnight field

---

[9] The first two stanzas of *LP* 30 are a free translation of the sixty-second poem of Heine's *Lyrisches Intermezzo:* "Am Kreuzweg wird begraben" (Elster edition; Leipzig, 1890). See the note on the printer's copy of *LP* 30, page 136.

❦ PART FOUR ❧

The Printer's Copy of
A Shropshire Lad

T H E printer's copy of *A Shropshire Lad* is in the library of
Trinity College, Cambridge. It was within this library that one
of the earlier collections of Housman's first volume was founded,
a project of which he evidently approved, for on at least one
occasion (2 May 1914) he asked his publisher for copies of all
editions in stock to augment the library's collection. It was fitting
that when Housman was ready to dispose of the final manuscript
of *A Shropshire Lad* he should present it to the library of his college. With it he sent this letter to the curator:

Trinity College
3 March 1926[1]

DEAR ADAMS,

I enclose the MS of *A Shropshire Lad*. XXXV is missing, and
after XXXVI the numeration differs a good deal from the final
order, because while the book was printing I took out five pieces

[1] The date of Housman's letter may have some bearing on the date of the
publication of his first volume of poetry. The records as to the precise day are
defective. Apparently Housman's correspondence with his publisher, Kegan Paul,
Trench, Trübner & Co., has perished; at any rate it is not now in the possession
of that firm's successor, Routledge & Kegan Paul, Ltd. A note in the second
edition of *A Shropshire Lad* (Richards, 1898) gives the date of the first printing
as February 1896. It was probably late in February, and the date of Housman's
bequest was therefore very near the thirtieth anniversary of the first appearance of *A Shropshire Lad*.

and put in the three now numbered **XXXIV, XXXVII,** and **XLI,** which are together at the end.[2]

Yours sincerely

A. E. HOUSMAN

Unlike the printer's copy of *Last Poems,* which never reached the composing room, the eighty-three sheets of the Trinity College MS. R. 1.91 show abundant evidence of the use for which they were designed. Ink smears and compositors' scrawled signatures adorn nearly every sheet, many leaves have been crudely folded, and a half-dozen of the first and last are ragged from handling. However, no portion of the manuscript has been lost and everything Housman wrote on it is legible, even if some of his notations are hardly intelligible.

The manuscript sheets measure 8″ x 11⅝″. They were originally ruled in blue ink, which has almost completely faded on a fourth of the pages. A. E. H. wrote throughout in black ink except where he jotted down tentative alternatives in pencil. If these were later approved, they were carefully traced over in ink and the rejected readings canceled with a horizontal line or two. The handwriting—about twice the size of the fair copy in his poetry notebooks—shows a careful, almost painful rotundity as if every word had been inscribed by a man acquainted with grief arising from printers' misreadings.

There are no corrections on the two pages of the Table of Contents, which A. E. H. evidently made up from page proof, for it is identical with the Table of Contents printed in the *editio princeps*. Seventeen[3] of the sixty-three poems were sent in with titles; but in his manuscript Table he ignored these captions, invariably referring to the poems by the first line (or a portion

[2] In the manuscript as it exists at present, these three pieces have not been shifted; they follow the final poem in the order 41, 37, 34. There were once eighty-four sheets (counting the Table of Contents and *ASL* 35); and beginning with *ASL* 1 these bear numerals (seemingly in Housman's hand) in the upper right corner. However, many of these have been crossed out and others put in, and midway in the manuscript these changes and shifts have made the numerical sequence somewhat bewildering. For example, what is now the forty-ninth sheet of poetry was originally number 64, later 51. In locating the poems by pages in the notes that follow, I have simply adopted the sequence of the poems as they now occur in the manuscript.

[3] Not counting "The Sage to the Young Man," withheld in proofreading.

thereof) of each. Throughout the manuscript there are some ninety discrepancies in punctuation between Housman's usage in the printer's copy and the reading of the text. These, and occasional variations in language, must be explained by alterations injected into the proof sheets. On these and other relevant matters the letters that passed between Housman and the first publisher of his timidly ventured book would make interesting reading. Even though this correspondence has dropped out of sight, it is not impossible that a portion of it may eventually be recovered. It seems unlikely that A. E. H. himself would have destroyed all the letters he received relating to his first volume.

In his letter of bestowal to Mr. Adams, Housman speaks of taking out five pieces. These were originally numbers 28, 33, 34, 42, and 43; and each but one has its history:

Number 28 was "In the morning, in the morning." Though once a part of the manuscript, the copy of this poem never left Housman's hands. He laid it by and twenty-six years later refurbished it for *Last Poems,* where it became number 23. The original *Shropshire Lad* copy, still bearing its original numeral, is now sheet 136 of the Library of Congress manuscripts.

The original copy of number 33 was also withdrawn from the manuscript. The poem itself I have not been able to identify, but it was probably one of the few unnumbered poems A. E. H. copied out with the others whose election was sure. The copies of three of these rejects now constitute sheets 135, 141, and 142 of the Library of Congress collection;[4] all were published in one or the other of the two posthumous volumes.

Number 34 was "Yonder see the morning blink." As with number 28, the copy of this poem never reached the composing room; it is now sheet 146 of the Library of Congress manuscripts. The poem survived to become number 11 of *Last Poems.*

The manuscript copy of number 42, "The Sage to the Young Man," passed on into the first proof sheets. The X-canceled manuscript, headed XLII, now exists in sheets 139 and 140 of the Library of Congress collection. A. E. H. again turned thumbs down on this lyric in assembling copy for *Last Poems*; it appeared as number 4 of *More Poems.*

[4] For titles of these poems see page 4 of this volume.

Number 43 was "Her strong enchantments failing." It, like number 42, was canceled in proofreading. The original *ASL* copy is not with the others in the Library of Congress remains; but, according to John Carter,[5] the proof sheet containing the poem has survived. Housman thought better of this lyric as he was readying his second volume and put it in as number 3 there.

Except for one mutual shift in the positions of lyrics 3 and 4, the arrangement of the first twenty-two poems in his printer's copy, as Housman first assembled it, was exactly in the order they were to carry in print. Number 4, "Reveille," had originally been headed 3, with "The Recruit" intended to follow. But before numbering the latter, the poet apparently reflected that though there is nothing soldierly in "Reveille" good military order required a poem carrying that name to come after "The Recruit"; so he triple-canceled his numeral III and changed it to IV. At one stage in the preparation of *A Shropshire Lad*, it may be recalled, Housman and his publisher considered a plan of presenting the poems as an appeal to the patriotic spirit. The arrangement of the first few poems in the volume is a vestige of this idea, which fortunately was dropped.

In the upper left corner of the page on which the thirteenth lyric appears ("When I was one-and-twenty") Housman wrote *"Another Series."* This caption may indicate that he had in mind a grouping of the next few poems here under a new theme, for the thirteenth, fourteenth, fifteenth, and sixteenth lyrics deal with a subject not hitherto expressed: the lover's sorrow after giving his heart away.

The following catalog includes all significant variations between the manuscript and the Kegan Paul edition, excepting punctuation. There, the main difference is in the larger number of commas added to the proof sheets—seventy-five more by actual count. These props may be taken as the author's concessions to editorial demands for "easier reading." Only four punctuation signs carried in the manuscript were canceled in proof; there were thirteen substitutions, commas for semicolons, and the like. Poem number 56, "The Day of Battle," appeared in print within quotation marks, but no such indication shows in the written copy.

[5] See *Library*, June 1942, p. 42.

Why were the signs of quotation added? Probably as a movement of retreat from the immediacy of the grim statement of the lyric (often left out even from the "soldiers' anthologies"). A similar motive may have been behind the use of quotation marks about the heretical lyric number 47, "The Carpenter's Son." Although A. E. H. after plainly heading stanza one with the sign of quotation inadvertently omitted all the rest, they do appear in their proper places throughout the printed text.

Many of the manuscript copies conform exactly or very nearly to print, and in the list that follows these are not mentioned.

1. "1887." On pages 1 and 2. Line 17: *tombstones shew*. The manuscript has this archaic or provincial spelling of the verb, which would have made a dubious rhyme with *overflow,* in line 19. In his letters and other prose Housman habitually preferred *shew*; but although he probably pronounced the word "show," it is strange that he did not perceive its slight inappropriateness here or in the draft on B 19, from which he made this copy.

vaulted

4. "Reveille." On page 6. Line 5: *the* ~~roof of~~ *shadow shatters.*

12. "When I watch the living meet." On page 17. Line 15: *And the bridegroom*. The third word here betrays the only verbal slip in the copying of the manuscript. Housman first wrote *bridge*; then, crowding his letters, spelled *bridegroom*.

14. "There pass the careless people." On page 19. Line 10: *From Thule to Cathay*. The Kegan Paul edition reads *Beneath the blue of day*—one of the many substitutions made in proofreading. On page 101 of Notebook B, after all but one of the lyrics of *A Shropshire Lad* had been finished, A. E. H. wrote among six other memos for correction the line *Beneath the blue of day,* which was the line he wanted for *ASL* 14:10.[6] However, his fondness for suggestive place-names must have made him forget or forgo the line, which only an eleventh-hour substitution sent into print.

15. "Look not in my eyes." On page 20. Line 14: *With downward eye*
gazes
and ~~bearing~~ *sad*. Housman's original copy of the line was verbatim from the unique notebook draft of the poem on A 232.

[6] This list is given on page 68.

cressy

20. "Oh fair enough are sky and plain." On page 26. Line 11: *the rushy brink*. The word *rushy* was carried over from the unique notebook copy on B 77.

23. "The lads in their hundreds." On page 30. Line 5: *There's men from the town* . . . In the printed text the second word in the line is *chaps*. This poem was originally listed as number 30; Housman may have shifted it in order to have a poem of more substance between 22 and the one first numbered 23, which have only twelve lines each.

24. "Say, lad, have you things to do?" On page 31. This number, first intended to be in the twenty-third place, was necessarily raised to 24 when 30 was interposed. The original number 24 appeared as number 33 in print.

28. "The Welsh Marches." On pages 36 and 37. Line 3: *her steepled crest*. The first edition reads *the steepled crest*. This poem was once number 29, but was set back to 28 when the lyric "In the morning, in the morning," first copied under that numeral, was withdrawn. The original sheet is now number 136 of the Library of Congress collection.

29. "The Lent Lily." On page 38. Originally number 30, this poem was lowered to position 29 in the shift affecting the preceding number.

30. "Others, I am not the first." On page 39. Line 14: *Blows no wind* . . . This was the reading of the revised draft on A 238, where the poem was composed. In making printer's copy from it Housman evidently forgot that in the corrigenda table on B 101 he had altered *Blows* to *Plays*. However, as with *ASL* 14:10, memory revived in proofreading, and the first edition carried *Plays no wind* . . . It is worthy of remark that the numeral XXX above this poem was never altered, proving that A. E. H. decided to reject his original twenty-eighth lyric almost immediately after making printer's copy for it. This decision *in medias res* provides an insight into the poet's critical judgment during the preparation of his manuscript.

31. "On Wenlock Edge." On page 40. Line 3 and line 17: *The wind* . . . The printed text has *The gale* . . . Housman copied *The wind* . . . from page 98 of his second notebook, but in the table on B 101 left a memo of the substitution that he sent into print while reading proof.

33. "If truth in hearts that perish." On page 42. The original number was 24; it was canceled and altered to 33. The poem first intended to be 33 is the second of the five rejected poems and the one lost number.

34. "The New Mistress." On page 81. This poem and "Yonder see the morning blink" were composed at about the same time and just in time for one of them to get into the complete manuscript of *A Shropshire Lad*. The only drafts of them in the notebooks exist on pages 114 and 116, respectively, of Notebook B, the later dated "Dec. '95." Having sent in "Yonder see the morning blink,"[7] Housman later repented of his choice and dispatched "The New Mistress" to replace it. This is the only *quid pro quo* insertion of the three poems that were put in while the manuscript was at the printer's.

In the upper left of the page that bore the substitute 34, A. E. H. wrote boldly "A Shropshire Lad"—a guide to the printer for the proper handling of the poem and the two others that probably went with it.

37. "As through the wild green hills of Wyre." On pages 79 and 80. This is another of the trio of inserted pieces. It was not intended to replace another poem, and in sending it in as number 37 Housman must have known that his manuscript already had one lyric under that numeral. This poem is mentioned immediately below.

38. "The winds out of the west land blow." On page 44. This poem was once number 40, but A. E. H. had relocated it as number 37 before the complete manuscript was ready. In his manuscript Table of Contents he correctly located his new number 37 and set "The winds . . ." in the next position following.

Line 10: *Thick on the wind* . . . The Kegan Paul edition has this reading, which Housman passed on from his latest draft of the poem, on B 58. However, in later editions the phrase was altered to *Loose on the wind*. One of the notable features in Housman's poetic growth is the improvement of his ear.

       Oh

Line 13: ~~My~~ *lads, at home I heard you plain.*

Line 18: *neither long could stay.* The printed text is *neither long abode.*

Line 20: *sigh upon the way.* The printed text is *sigh upon the road.* For the final versions of lines 18 and 20 the poet went back to his first draft of the lyric, on A 233.

[7] The withdrawn copy of this poem, bearing the numeral XXXIV, is sheet 146 of the Library of Congress manuscripts.

The Printer's Copy of *A Shropshire Lad*

39. " 'Tis time, I think, by Wenlock town." On page 45. This poem was once number 43 but went off in the manuscript as number 38. The shift affecting the two preceding pieces finally set this poem in the thirty-ninth place.

> *will*
>
> Line 12: *That ~~shall~~ not shower on me.*

40. "Into my heart an air that kills." On page 46. This poem was once number 41, altered to 39. Like its two immediate predecessors, this poem was eventually moved up one position in the Table of Contents.

It may be worthy of remark that, so far as we may judge by the evidences in the notebooks, this is the first poem of *A Shropshire Lad* in order of composition. From his corrected ink draft on A 63, Housman wrote printer's copy for this lyric.

41. "In my own shire, if I was sad." On page 77. Line 22: *No such comrades* . . . The printed text has *No such helpmates.* This poem is the third and last of the interjected pieces. It was an out-and-out addition and since it replaced nothing, the manuscript had two poems numbered 41 when it arrived.

42. "The Merry Guide." On pages 47, 48, and 49. The manuscript shows the number of this poem, once 51, changed to 40. A. E. H. made this copy from the ink draft on pages 114 and 115 of his first notebook, dated "Sept. 1890." There was an earlier draft, in pencil, under the same date on pages 106 and 107 and an intermediate ink draft on pages 108 and 109. The proximity of these three copies proves Housman's absorption in this poem; and his measured, flawless writing of the printer's copy of "The Merry Guide" attests that every word of it was set down *con amore.*

43. "The Immortal Part." On pages 50 and 51. This poem was first number 59, but was set back to 41, and again moved to forty-third place.

> *brain*
>
> Line 11: *This ~~mind~~ that fills the skull* . . .
>
> Line 15: *bones must brook control.* The first edition here reads *bones obey control.*
>
> Line 17: *'Tis time that eves and morns were gone.* The printed text is *'Tis long till eve and morn are gone.*
>
> *Lie down in the bed of dust*
>
> Line 25: ~~To bed, to bed; lie down in dust.~~

The next poem in the manuscript Housman sent to the printer was headed thus:

XLII
~~XLIV~~

The sage to the young man.

The poem following this was "Her strong enchantments failing." As has already been mentioned, A. E. H. suppressed both of these pieces.

46. "Bring, in this timeless grave to throw." On page 55. Once number 35, this poem was changed to number 46 before the manuscript went to the printer's.

Line 12: *Straws the last gleaner overstept.* Housman struck out the first word of this line and wrote *Awns* in front.

50. "In valleys of springs of rivers." On page 60. The manuscript shows this poem as number 51. The traditional quatrain at the beginning of the printed text is not in the manuscript copy but was added in proof-reading.[8] The poet had written it between stanzas two and three on B 40, where the poem was begun.

52. "Far in a western brookland." On page 62. This poem was once 55, later 54. The phrase *long since forgotten* in the ninth line of the manuscript and in the printed text was subsequently altered to *no more remembered.*

53. "The True Lover." On pages 63 and 64. The manuscript shows this poem as number 55.

       Light was the air

Line 15: ~~*The air was light*~~ *beneath the sky.* Housman's latest notebook draft of this poem, on A 212–13, shows that he had wrestled with every other line of the stanza (the fourth) but this one.

---

[8] The stanza, which is sometimes taken for Housman's, runs thus:

> Clunton and Clunbury,
>   Clungunford and Clun,
> Are the quietest places
>   Under the sun.

In the third line instead of *quietest,* tradition would have allowed A. E. H. to choose among *sleepiest, drunkenest, dirtiest,* and perhaps a few others even more uncomplimentary.

55. "Westward on the high-hilled plains." On page 66. In the manuscript this poem is number 57.

Line 9: *There, when ~~ashen~~ is the west.*

> *hueless*

58. "When I came last to Ludlow." On page 69. The manuscript shows this heading, first written in pencil and then carefully inked over: "The Return of the Native." The borrowed title was evidently canceled in proofreading.[9]

62. "Terence, this is stupid stuff." On pages 73, 74, and 75. This poem was once number 64.

Line 13: *Or drive them melancholy mad.* The printed text is *Moping melancholy mad.*

Line 46: *Good's a chance but ill is sure.* The printed text reads *Luck's a chance, but trouble's sure.*

63. "I hoed and trenched and weeded." On page 76. In the manuscript this poem is number 65. This discrepancy of two units in the numerals heading several of the latter poems is, finally, the result of Housman's last-minute withdrawal of five poems, adding but three. His manuscript contained originally sixty-five pieces; the Kegan Paul edition contained sixty-three.

---

[9] Housman's disinclination to use titles from other writers ("The Merry Guide" on A 106 carried for subtitle a phrase from Homer) has not been emulated by writers acquainted with his poetry. I have counted over forty books published since 1920 under titles picked up from Housman's poetry: four named *Angry Dust*, three *Shoulder the Sky*, etc.

❧ PART FIVE ❧

The Printer's Copy of *Last Poems*

GRANT RICHARDS, recalling his first glimpse into the fifty-page manuscript of *Last Poems,* exclaims with an enthusiasm touched with a gleam of omnipathy: "Yes, the greatest moment in my life as a publisher was when I opened the sheaf of manuscript that was *Last Poems.* . . . I will go further and say that no publisher alive has had a greater thrill."[1] This was on the evening of 20 June 1922. Richards' secretary began making a typescript of the poems the following morning. The book itself was published almost exactly four months later, and on November 1 Housman presented his manuscript of *Last Poems* to the Fitzwilliam Museum, at Cambridge.[2] With it he addressed this letter to the director, his friend Sydney Cockerell:

Note: This chapter was originally published in the *Papers of the Bibliographical Society of America,* volume 46, First Quarter 1952. Reprinted by permission.

[1] *Housman, 1897–1936,* p. 195. It is from Grant Richards' gossipy but useful memoir, pp. 191–201, that most of the data in reference to the publication of *Last Poems* have been drawn. The confession quoted above was first made in his *Author Hunting* (London: Hamilton, 1934), p. 267.

[2] In making this bequest Housman may have had in mind one of his manuscripts already in the Fitzwilliam: a draft of "R. L. S.," which had been given to the Museum 11 May 1920 by Ralph Griffin, F.S.A. According to A. S. F. Gow (*A. E. Housman, A Sketch,* p. 22), the poet objected to the exhibition of this lyric (for which his liking had cooled) and asked that it be restored to him. Gow is not quite correct in saying that "when he gave the museum the manuscript of *Last Poems* he retrieved and burnt the poem he wished forgotten," for the manuscript of "R. L. S." did not come into Housman's hands again until 1 May 1924, a year and a half after he had made his bequest.

The Printer's Copy of *Last Poems*

Trinity College
1 November 1922

DEAR COCKERELL:

As I still cannot lay my hands on the *Shropshire Lad* MS, and as you are more ardent for possession than the College Library, I send the MS of *Last Poems*. Half-a-dozen pieces are missing. The MS, as you will see, did not go to the printers but a type-written copy was made in the publisher's office.

Yours sincerely

A. E. HOUSMAN

This swift routing of the manuscript from Housman's desk to his publisher's, back to the author, and thence to the Fitzwilliam, with no stopover at the printing house, was to posterity's advantage; for nearly every one of the forty-five sheets is in "mint" condition. Unlike the printer's copy of *A Shropshire Lad,* which went where it was intended and received its full due of thumb smudges, this final draft of *Last Poems* now looks about as it did just after Housman put the last period on the last page. His publisher had suggested that it would be necessary to prepare for the printer a typewritten copy of the manuscript, and to this arrangement Housman had agreed—not without the whimsical protest that "it [the typewriting] will not be more legible than the hand I write literature in." However, Grant Richards' first look at the manuscript must have caused him to give thanks that his author had yielded the point, for the rotund, easy style of the poet's early hand is not present here. There are several evidences of hasty penmanship that produced errors later crudely corrected by pen strokes or overwriting. In many of the pages the script is somewhat cramped or sketchy. No compositor not an expert in Housman's calligraphy could have been safely trusted with it.

All this is not to say that, so far as the *matter* of the pages is concerned, this copy was made with less than the meticulous care the poet habitually gave to such tasks. Thanks to pains taken, the agreement between his copy and the text of the first edition is nearly perfect, even by his standards. There are—to be painfully exact—only eight variations in punctuation between Housman's manuscript and the first printing, and none of these are important. There are but four verbal discrepancies (which

131

may be accounted for by substitutions made later in proofreading), and one of these is a mere inadvertence in spelling *forlorn*. In his Preface to *Last Poems* Housman mentions his solicitude for these minutiae in launching his final book of poetry, declaring, "What I have written should be printed while I am here to see it through the press and control its spelling and punctuation." If things did not come out right in print, the ones to blame were the "filthy beasts" who "corrected" his copy. And blamed they were, in language as scorching as the epithets Housman the Latinist used to blast the German editors of Manilius.

The pages of the manuscript measure $7\frac{1}{4}''$ x $12\frac{1}{4}''$. They are numbered in the upper right corner, with no numerals above the poems. All the pages are ruled horizontally in light blue ink and eight have a left hand marginal rule. Housman wrote throughout in black ink, using a rather coarse pen. There is no Table of Contents in the manuscript.

In his letter of transmittal to Sydney Cockerell, the poet remarks that half-a-dozen pieces are missing. Actually only five sheets seem to be absent: numbers 5, 14, 19, 21, and 43. Five poems are missing: 3, 15, 17, 18, and 22; and as luck would have it a late but not final draft of one of these poems (number 3) is reproduced opposite page 196 in Grant Richards' memoir. It is certain that the five missing sheets were not, in whole or in part, sent to the British Museum; three *Last Poems* holographs are preserved there, but they are of poems 12, 33, and 35.[3] In the notes that follow, something will be said as to the identity of these five "lost" poems and other possible discards from the manuscript.

The order of the lyrics in the printed book was a matter of more than secondary importance to the author. On June 15 he took this problem up with his publisher: "I cannot arrange the order of the poems satisfactorily until I know for certain which I shall include and which omit; and on that point, as I told you, I want to consult one or two people. Therefore I want the poems

[3] These are fair copies, slightly corrected, that Laurence Housman presented to the keeper of manuscripts, 13 June 1936, through Professor G. M. Trevelyan. I have been informed by Carl Winter, director of the Fitzwilliam Museum, that numbers 3, 17, and 22 were offered (by an anonymous person) at Sotheby's on 28 April 1937. They are now in a private collection in America. See page 50 of the Carter and Sparrow *Hand-List* (London: Rupert Hart-Davis, 1952).

printed first simply according to the various metres they are written in, not at all as they will afterwards stand. Will the transposition which will then have to be made before the book arrives at its proper form be very expensive? If so, perhaps type-writing had better be used, but I do not like it, as it makes things look repulsive."

But by the time the copy was ready to send off, Housman was more confident of finality: "I do not think much transposition will be required," he observed in the note that accompanied the complete manuscript on June 19. As a matter of fact, the numbering of his pages agrees precisely with the sequence of print as far as page 20 of the manuscript, which contains the sixteenth poem. On July 10, returning corrected proofs, Housman sent in his one additional poem, which was 17 or 18 (two of the five pieces now missing). With this insertion came directions for some rearrangements, which are specified in my notes that follow. The great thing in the sequence of the pieces of his second volume is the effect of the concluding three poems, which rise one after the other into a climax of exquisitely tuned music that has no parallel in Housman's poetry and few in others'.

In the following list (as in Part Four), copies that do not vary significantly from the printed text of the first edition are not mentioned unless some peculiarity justifies it.

Prologue poem. "We'll to the woods no more." Line 10: *leavy woods*. This older spelling was abandoned in proofreading, and the first edition has *leafy woods*.

At the right of his page Housman drew a long enclosing line and wrote: "Italics, and smaller print than the rest." Though Richards objected to the smaller type, the first edition shows he followed orders. It is worth noting that the only anterior draft for this poem that has survived in Housman's notebooks carries the title "Nous n'irons plus aux bois," quoted from a fifteenth-century *ronde*. Having decided that "We'll to the woods no more" was to be the title poem for the book, Housman concluded that the poem itself should be left untitled.[4]

[4] This chapter when it appeared in the *Papers of the Bibliographical Society of America* stated that a period was "inadvertently omitted in the ms." at the end of line 8 of *LP* 1. Such was the evidence of the photoduplicate which I was using. However, I learned from the anonymous reviewer in the *London Times Literary Supplement* that the original manuscript clearly showed the period; and

3. "Her strong enchantments failing." Not in the manuscript; probably on the missing fifth sheet. The facsimile opposite page 196 of Richards' memoir, although it is entitled "A Page from the Original Manuscript of *Last Poems*," does not appear to be a representation of the missing sheet, as no ruled lines are to be seen. The Richards facsimile shows line 2 thus: *Her woven toils in wreck*; the second and third words were line-canceled by the poet, and *towers of fear* written above, bringing the poem to the finality of print. This poem had been intended to be 43 of *A Shropshire Lad*; but it was canceled in the proofsheets.

5. "Grenadier." On page 7. Line 8: ~~can~~ *shall* *march*. This substitute word (like others of its kind throughout the manuscript) was written in pencil, later retraced in ink.

6. "Lancer." On page 8. Line 9: Housman absently wrote *by lying*, then bearing on his pen, blurred the first word to *be*.

8. "Soldier from the wars returning." On page 10. At the end of line 5 the manuscript shows a semicolon; the printed text has a comma. In line 13 a comma omitted after the first *you* was added in proofreading.

9. "The chestnut casts his flambeaux." On page 11. This is the first of the poems about which Housman, comparing his new volume to *A Shropshire Lad,* dropped this warning to his publisher: ". . . it [*Last Poems*] had better have a wider page, or smaller print, or both, as there are more poems in it which have long lines." There are no variations between the manuscript and print.

11. "Yonder see the morning blink." On page 13. This poem was once intended to be 34 of *A Shropshire Lad*. The withdrawn copy is sheet 146 of the Library of Congress manuscripts. It shows many corrections and alternative readings, indicating that twenty-six years earlier the author had gone to more than usual pains to ready it for his first volume. The *Last Poems* copy shows no variations from print.

The sheet that bore the numeral 14 is the second of the five missing ones. As the following sheet contains the next poem to be printed—number 12—it seems probable that page 14 of the manuscript contained a poem which Housman decided later to take out. It very likely was one of the nine unsuccessful candidates for printer's copy (now included in

this fact has since been confirmed by an official of the Fitzwilliam Museum. In, damned spot!

the Library of Congress Volume VI) or one of two poems drafted in Notebook D and later scored with the long diagonal line that was the sign of final copy: "The stars have not dealt me the worst they could do" (D 48) and "Stone, steel, dominions pass" (D 66).[5]

15. "Eight O'Clock." Not in the manuscript; probably on page 19, also missing here.

17. "Astronomy." 18. "The rain, it streams on stone and hillock." The copies of these two poems are not in the manuscript. One or the other of them may have occupied page 21, which likewise is absent. Either 17 or 18 was the one addition Housman sent to his publisher after delivering the packet of final copy. Both of these poems point toward the death of the poet's younger brother, George Herbert; and it may have been that Housman decided only at the eleventh hour to return to this theme, already touched in "Illic Jacet"—number 4.

19. "In midnights of November." On page 22. Line 18: instead of *forlorn* Housman absently wrote *folorn,* which was never corrected.

21. "The fairies break their dances." On page 30. The forward shift of this poem was evidently one of the few rearrangements the poet asked for in a letter dated July 10, accompanying the corrected proof sheets.

22. "The sloe was lost in flower." There is no copy for this number; it may have been on the missing forty-third page.

23. "In the morning, in the morning." On page 24. This poem was the last of the three pieces once numbered for *A Shropshire Lad* but later withdrawn; the rejected draft (headed **XXVIII**) is now sheet 136 of the Library of Congress manuscripts. Only one line there (number 5) shows a variation from the copy made for *Last Poems,* which passed into print exactly as we now read it.

25. "The Oracles." On page 29. This poem was moved out of its original position, which was two places nearer the end. The first three lines of the last stanza the poet underlined, indicating italic type. The title "The Oracles" must have been the result of a last-minute decision, for the manuscript shows no heading; but the title "The Oracle" had appeared over the poem when it was published in the 1903 *Venture* (page 39), an annual edited by Laurence Housman and W. Somerset Maugham and published by John Bailie. The poem was probably copied from page

---

[5] These two lyrics were published as *AP* 17 and *MP* 24.

202 of Notebook B, but there the title of the piece is "Delphi and Thermopylae." This is another of the long-line poems, and Housman's copy of it shows no broken lines, the longest ones ending neatly near the right margin—an encouragement to the printer to follow copy, which he did not do.

28. "Now dreary dawns the eastern light." On page 32. This poem and the one following changed places in going from manuscript to print.

30. "Sinner's Rue." On page 33. Line 7: *the* ~~flower~~ *weed*. Line 13: *healing*
of ~~saining~~. Above this poem Housman wrote a title from Heine, *Die Armesuenderblume*, then crossed it out with a heavy pen and superscribed *Sinner's rue*.

31. "Hell Gate." On pages 34, 35, 36, and 37. The only correction in the copy of this, Housman's longest poem, occurs in line 68, where he canceled *swarm* and wrote above it *hive*.

32. "When I would muse in boyhood." On page 38. Line 2: the comma at the end of the line in the Richards edition does not occur in the manuscript.

33. "When the eye of day is shut." On page 39. Lines 1, 2: at the ends of these lines there are no commas as in the printed text. Line 3: *the hunter's hut*. The manuscript shows no alternative; and it must have been in the proofreading that Housman changed *hunter's* to *forest*, thus departing from the reading he had taken from page 45 of his third notebook, the immediate source for this poem.

34. "The First of May." On page 40. Line 20: *Stands upright on the dead*. This was the first reading, but Housman line-canceled the second word and superscribed *lofty*. This word evidently passed into the proof sheets where it later gave way to *planted*, which was probably a reminiscence from a single line written long ago on page 139 of his second notebook: *Planted deep on perished people*. The title seems also to have been added by afterthought, for it is crowded near the upper margin of the manuscript page; all the other captions in the manuscript are written comfortably down on one of the first four lines.

36. "Revolution." On page 42. The title by which readers know the poem is not in Housman's copy; there is none for it in the first edition or in the five other printings of 1922. The poet named this lyric in a

letter to Grant Richards dated 28 January 1926, granting permission to the headmaster of Winchester College to use the poem in an anthology: ". . . and if he wants a title he can call it 'Revolution,' which may be of use, as most readers do not seem to see that it is a parable."

The next sheet in the manuscript (number 43) is the last of the missing five. It may have contained a rejected poem, or possibly the missing poem 22.

40. "Tell me not here." On page 48, which was by error also numbered 47. Line 10: *leavy dells.* Here the poet again preferred the archaic spelling of the adjective, as he had in the prologue poem.

41. "Fancy's Knell." On pages 49 and 50. Lines 2 and 15: the printed commas at the ends of these lines are not in the manuscript; nor is the Shakespearean title. Uniquely here, the individual stanzas were headed by Arabic numerals, later canceled by diagonal pen strokes.

Index of Titles and First Lines

THIS index refers to (1) the poetry collected for the first time in this volume, complete poems and separate quatrains, and (2) poems quoted or cited from the standard Holt edition.

Index of Titles and First Lines

Index of Titles and First Lines

General Index

Abandoned lines and stanzas, 95–119
Academy, ix, 24
Additional Poems: publication of, 5, 6; contents of, 7, 8; incorporated with *Collected Poems,* 8; contribution of Notebook A to, 19; *No. 1,* 11; *No. 2,* 11, 26; *No. 4,* 104; *No. 5,* 8, 11; *No. 6,* 11, 85; *No. 7,* 11; *No. 10,* 67; *No. 11,* 36; *No. 12,* 8; *No. 13,* 8, 11; *No. 14,* 8; *No. 17,* 135; *No. 18,* ix, 4, 21; *No. 19,* 8, 11, 45; *No. 20,* 8, 11, 69; *No. 21,* 8, 11; *No. 22,* 8, 100, 130; *No. 23,* x, 8, 20, 22, 80, 112
Adhesive on notebook sheets, 10, 12
A. E. Housman, A Sketch, 130
A. E. Housman, An Annotated Hand-List, 132
Alternative readings, 31, 68, 80, 95, 134
"Analysis" of the notebooks, 8–9, 12, 17, 22, 25, 28, 39, 50, 51
Angry Dust, 129
Arnold, Matthew, 68
Author Hunting, 130

"Barbed criticisms," 51, 76
"Beech Tree" poem, 29, 87, 94
Biblical phrases, 40
Boer War, 24
British Museum, 132
Buried Life, A, 16

Cancellations in manuscripts, 10, 29, 31, 95
Carter, John, x, 132

Chronology of the manuscripts, ix–x
Cockerell, Sir Sydney, ix, 22, 25, 69, 79, 81, 130
Collamore, A. B., 15
Collected Poems of A. E. Housman, The: publication of, x, 8; poems not represented in L.C. collection, 11; "God's Acre," 36
Compound epithets, 35, 47, 64
Corrections in printer's copy, 124, 131, 134
Cutting of manuscripts, 9–10, 17, 19, 20, 22, 24, 81, 91, 108

Dates in notebooks, ix–x, 12, 14, 16, 18, 20, 22, 25, 26, 29, *et seq.*
"Dream poem," 29

Eliot, George, 93
Etudes Anglaises, 91

Fitzwilliam Museum, 130, 134
Foolscap manuscript sheets, xii, 4–5, 8, 11: abandoned lines and stanzas, 117–19
"Fred Loughton," 23

Gow, A. S. F., 130
Griffin, Ralph, 130

Heine, Heinrich, 119, 136
Housman, A. E.: provisions of his will, 3, 6, 9; destroys draft of *ASL 63,* 5, 11; exaggerations in Preface of *LP,* 15–16,

144

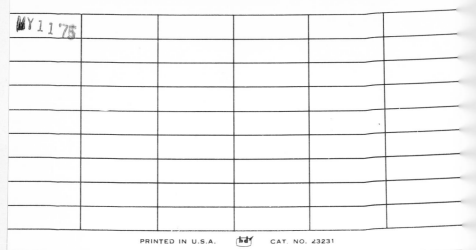